Enrichment Games

for High-Energy Dogs

Barbara Buchmayer

OTHER BOOKS BY BARB BUCHMAYER
Positive Herding 101: Dog-friendly Training
Positive Herding 201: Advanced Dog Training
More information can be found at *www.positiveherdingdog.com*.

Copyright © 2023 Barbara Buchmayer
Library of Congress Control Number: 2023906204

First published in 2023 by Positive Herding 101, LLC
14649 Hwy M, Purdin, MO 64674

To purchase a copy of this book or to sign up for news from Barb, please go to *www.enrichmentgames.com/*. To see online Enrichment Games courses, visit *https://enrichmentgames.com/eg-course*.

PHOTOGRAPHS
Sally Adam/Pam Eloff: pp 1, 3, 76, 83, 85 | Judy Albrecht Richmond: p 11 | Laurie Burbank: pp 13, 25, 37, 53, 95, 107, 129, 156, 159, back cover | Paula Stone: p 86 | Loretta Jakubiec: p 117 | Clean Run: back cover (Just Be Ewe Bungee Tug) | Barbara Buchmayer: all other images

Typography by User Friendly, Cape Town, South Africa
Set in Zapf Humanist 10.5 on 15pt

ISBN (print color softcover): 978-1-7368443-7-3
ISBN (epub): 978-1-7368443-3-5

Contents

Ready, set ... Game on!

The rules of the game

General rules

1. Fun first!
2. Give a cue only once.
3. Mark with a word or click, pause, and then reinforce with a treat or toy.
4. Break games into smaller steps when you or your dog struggles.
5. Keep game sessions short.
6. Safety always!

To win: Winning will be defined for each game.

Level up: How to level up for each game.

Challenge: (To be filled in later!)

_____

_____

_____

More information on the rules is found in the following chapter.

CHAPTER 1

Let's change your dog's life!

This is the book that you asked me to write, well not you exactly, but someone very much like you. Or maybe it was your dog, your high-energy dog.

Then again, maybe it was the gal who asked a question during one of my webinars. Let's call her Laura and her dog Sam, which are not their real names. "I have a dog", she began, "who is extremely distractable. He listens well in my house and is pretty good in any indoor setting, but … as soon as we go outside he becomes totally distracted. Lose your mind distracted. He cannot sit or down, although he is proficient in doing both when inside. There is no way I could ever let him off-lead outside as I would have no hope of recalling him. I don't think he can even hear me in this situation, much less respond. What can I do?" she pleaded.

*Sir playing an **advanced** enrichment game.*

Since I faced a similar situation with one of my dogs many years ago, I knew just how desperate she was. Her question brought back gut-wrenching memories but it also made me realize that I could suggest a simple solution that most likely would work for her. The solution begins with a game, an enrichment game.

Your dog

Before I tell you how I answered Laura's question, let's talk specifically about your dog, the Energizer Bunny dog, whose energy never seems to run down. You take your dog on a long walk or repeatedly throw a ball or Frisbee and they are ready for more. Let them run on a sandy beach or climb a steep mountain trail and they seem to grow stronger as your energy flags.

Let's face it, you are going to tire out long before your dog does. So how about presenting them with a challenging mental puzzle? Afterward, they may take a 5-minute nap, or not. What's a person to do?

Having lived with border collies for decades, I know what it is like to co-exist with high-energy dogs. Some days they get sufficient exercise and enrichment in their lives and some days not. Even with the best of intentions, it is difficult to provide the mental and physical stimulation that high-energy dogs need.

My dogs normally chill when inside, but I know that they would often love more activity in their days, even though they live on a farm and usually enjoy long walks daily. But a good walk or a run doesn't wear a dog out. Throwing a ball or toy for a dog to retrieve may take the edge off but may not be the best plan and usually doesn't provide significant mental exercise.

Using a tug as the reinforcer for a cone game that starts simple but grows in complexity.

Over the years, I have looked at mental exercises for dogs and canine enrichment activities, but most of them focus primarily on mental stimulation. Brain games are great, but dogs need to burn physical energy too. There just wasn't much out there that provided mental *and* physical enrichment for dogs, until now!

The gap

While teaching basic dog-sport skills to my dogs, I serendipitously developed games that fill this mind/body exercise void. These are games that provide both mental and physical stimulation for your dog while simultaneously teaching essential skills. Could your dog benefit from increased self-control, sharpened listening skills, and a stronger bond with you? The best part is that as these games become more challenging for your dog, they become easier for you.

Enrichment games can even be played inside, if you have enough room.

After playing these games with my dogs for many years, I shared them with other owners of active dogs. They had just as much success playing these games with their dogs as I did with mine. In fact, they and their dogs had so much fun that people watching wanted to learn how to play the games too!

So what is it exactly that makes these games so attractive? Imagine simple games that are a challenge, mentally and physically for your dog, but easy for you. Your dog gets tons of physical and mental enrichment as they play the games while you are able to move as much or as little as you desire. Not just any old boring games, but exciting games that have your dog completely engaged with you as together you build a no-regrets relationship.

Engagement versus Entertainment

Let's take a quick look at why you play enrichment games with your dog. Since most people don't make a distinction between an engaging activity and an entertaining one, that's where we will start. There are two types of activities that have been labeled as enrichment, those that enrich while you engage with your dog and those that enrich without your engagement. You set up the puzzle or snuffle mat but your dog interacts with it alone. Both activities are useful in different situations.

Engagement activities are done with your dog and they stimulate your dog mentally and physically. They also build your relationship and the communication skills between you and your dog. Entertainment activities are played by your dog alone. They are good as a short-term diversion or for older dogs or dogs recovering from an injury.

The difference between an entertainment activity and an engagement game is your level of participation.

This book contains engagement games that you play with your dog. By playing these games with your dog you build listening skills, improve self-control, and foster a stronger relationship.

New, unique games

Enrichment Games for High-Energy Dogs contains unique games that will transform your connection with your dog while providing tons of mental and physical exercise for your dog, but not so much for you. You can run and be active while playing these games or you can remain almost stationary.

Another great feature of these games is that you can easily match the level of the physical and mental challenge of the play to the degree of difficulty that is right for you and your dog. The games are easily modified as your and your dog's needs change day to day. The intensity of the play can also be quickly adapted to different dogs, changing physical needs, or the stages of a dog's life. These games are for all high-energy dogs, from youthful teens to seasoned golden oldies.

These games are for you and your dog if:
- Your dog loves to chase, run, or control movement.
- You want to mentally challenge your dog while you exercise their body.
- You want to build a stronger relationship with your dog.
- Your dog seems to have unlimited energy but you don't.

If you see yourself and your dog in the statements above, then these games are definitely for you!

The real world

There are also everyday advantages to playing enrichment games. Once your dog has learned the basic games, they will have acquired a level of self-control that will make your dog friends jealous!

The more you play these games, the more your dog will become tuned in to you and responsive to your cues. As you and your dog come together playing, your relationship will bloom. There is no better way to build an amazing relationship with your dog than by playing games together that are fun and captivating.

The bottom line

Let's jump to the bottom line. How are enrichment games different from other activities you do with your dog? First and most importantly, enrichment games are played primarily for the fun of playing. Period.

Second, dogs need to move and high-energy dogs not only need to move a lot, but they love to move fast. Throwing a ball or Frisbee may give your dog plenty of exercise, but this exercise can just be mindless chasing. Instead, these games provide quality mental and safe physical exercise for your dog.

Safe enrichment

Your high-energy dog must find ways to expend their energy. If you don't provide safe outlets for their excess energy, they will find other ways to burn their high-octane fuel. Left to their own devices, your dog may engage in behaviors that you may find undesirable or downright dangerous. If active dogs are confined to a house, crate, or small pen for extended periods, they may even injure or mutilate themselves.

Gold relaxing while I work in my office.

My dogs and I are happiest when they receive sufficient physical and mental stimulation every day. I see that their need for stimulation has been met when they happily nap or chill out while I putter around the house or work at my computer.

What are enrichment games?

Enrichment games, as I define them, are fun activities that spark curiosity, present attainable mental challenges, and provide physical exercise. If the activity or game is thoughtfully structured, it also helps to build a great relationship.

The complexity of these games can be increased as your dog builds skills or you can keep the play simple. You craft the games for your and your dog's specific needs. You can play indoors or out, fast or slow, add more behaviors and elements or stick to the basics. The games are totally customizable and easily adaptable to changing situations.

Ready to play?

Let's look at the training your dog needs to have mastered to successfully play these games. The skills your dog needs to have on cue are sit, down, and come. A retrieve will also come in very handy along the way. Most of the games can be adapted to treat tossing but a dog skilled at tugging will take to these games like a duck to water.

The beauty of these games is that they start simply and build from there. No fancy or expensive equipment is needed and a minimal amount of room. Since you will be exercising both your dog's mind and body, you won't need to play for extended periods, although your dog is not going to want to stop playing. Master a few enrichment games and you can look forward to a lifetime of enjoyment playing with your dog.

Let's change your dog's life!

Enrichment games use a step-by-step framework that allows you and your dog to advance at a comfortable pace. Move forward when both you and your dog are ready for a new, slightly more challenging game. The games are designed to be fun and engaging at all levels, from beginner through advanced.

Judy Albrecht Richmond and Ty playing a cone game.

Eleven enrichment games in a nutshell

Green grass games – the six basic games

1. Get on base – Introduce your dog to the joy of seeking a home base.
2. Run the bases – Get your dog moving inside or out with a simple target game.
3. Distraction action – Challenge your dog to respond to simple cues while you ramp up the distractions. This game tests your dog's ability to respond when the environment and your actions get distracting.
4. Engagement game – Now you are going to raise the ante a bit. Can your dog respond to you when they are focused on something else? Can they respond to you when they are moving away from you and toward something they are focused on?
5. Cone squares – Add circling and other actions to the Engagement game. Your dog's speed of movement starts to ramp up in this game.
6. Cone circles – Expanding the size of your cone circle and adding exciting elements are the focus of this challenging game. Further challenge your dog by creating unique games using low jumps, targets, and more.

Blue sky games – the five advanced games

7. **Flirt pole fun** – Learn the basics of handling and playing with a flirt pole. This is the game your dog won't want to miss!
8. **Squirrel on the loose** – Add the flirt pole to Cone squares. Simple but not easy.
9. **Go fish** – This game combines Cone circles with **Squirrel on the loose** for tons of fun. Add verbal cues, changes of direction, and a tape circle to keep your dog engaged with you as they play.

10. **Level up** – Level up by adding speed changes and moving into and back out of Cone circles. Increase the difficulty of play as your and your dog's skill sets soar.
11. **Blue sky** – The sky is the limit in this game. Any safe element you can imagine can be added to the Cone circles game. Think of two or three circles, tunnels, and figure 8s. The list is endless!

All of the enrichment games are mentally challenging for your dog. The physical challenges ramp up as the games move from your dog standing still to them moving at any safe speed that you desire, from a walk to a gallop.

Flirting with Sam

I don't want to leave Laura, Sam, or you hanging. My suggestion for helping Sam with his inability to engage with Laura when outside was twofold. First, I suggested that she have Sam checked out by a vet behaviorist to make sure that there wasn't some underlying problem that caused him to be so distracted by the outdoor sights, sounds, smells, and movements. I doubted that was Sam's problem, but better safe than sorry.

My primary suggestion was for her to play an enrichment game with Sam – the Cone circle game. This game can be played with treats, tugs, balls, or a flirt pole, which is a flexible pole with a toy attached to the end by a string. Since Sam was very into tugging while inside, I suggested she introduce him to indoor flirt pole play. Using a small flirt pole would allow her to play in quite a small area.

Because a flirt pole toy can be made to appear to run and jump, the toy can mimic prey. Prey is the one thing that most dogs get super engaged with. Thus, it is a good bet that she could get Sam engaged inside her house. Then she could transfer that engagement to other rooms in her home, her screened porch, and then outside. Initially, she would need to play in a fenced area or have a leash or long line on Sam. Eventually, she may even be able to give Sam some freedom when outdoors!

Did it work?

I can't tell you if my suggestion worked for Laura and Sam because we didn't stay in touch, but I want to make sure that your story has a happy ending by introducing you and your dog to some fun, stimulating games.

I can tell you that flirt pole play worked for me and my dog when I had the same situation that Laura is facing. Enrichment games can't solve every problem that your dog has but they can provide tons of mental and physical exercise for your dog while building a great relationship.

Welcome to *Enrichment Games for High-Energy Dogs: Your step-by-step guide to dog training fun!*

If you want to play amazingly fun games with your dog that provide cognitive, sensory, food, social, and physical enrichment, then this book is definitely for you.

Let the games begin!

LEVEL 1: GREEN GRASS GAMES

Cheat sheet #1

Get on base

1. Fun first!
2. Practice without your dog.
3. Mark, then treat as your dog moves closer and closer to the foot target/home base.
4. Mark, then treat dog standing on target.
5. Move dog around target by treat placement.
6. Move target around the floor.
7. Add hand signal (point).
8. Move target outdoors.
9. Get your dog running to seek the target.

To win: Dog runs directly to home base and stands on it.

Level up: When cued, dog runs directly to home base and stands on it.

Challenge: _____

_____

CHAPTER 2

Get on base

Before you jump into gameplay, I want to introduce two icons to help you navigate the book. These icons will direct your attention to either game plans or helpful hints.

Game plan: This icon is found at the start of a game plan or list. If you are looking for where to start a game, just search for this cute pup!

HINT: These are suggestions or ideas to make the games easier or to add a further explanation as needed. (Hints are also known as cheats.)

Get on base

I want to start by introducing a skill that will quickly get your dog moving to home base. A home base is just a target that your dog can stand on. Since you will start with only one base or target, you can think of this target as a home base for your dog. In the next game, Run the bases, you will be adding more targets or bases.

The Get on base game is an easy way to introduce your dog to gameplay. You will be using large targets, placed on the floor or ground. Possible targets include Frisbees, mats, low platforms, pieces of carpet, or foam squares. A target of about 2×3 feet is a nice size for large dogs. Smaller targets are fine, but your dog will have to be more precise when targeting them with their paws.

Since your dog will be standing on the target with their front paws, we will call these targets or bases – **foot targets**. Many types of targets, such as nose, hip, or head targets, are commonly used to indicate where a dog is to go or what they are to do. This game focuses on foot targets.

To get the game started you will work with only one target. Once your dog is happily seeking the target, you can add another target. Then you will get your dog moving from target to target. So how do you and your dog get started?

Pieces of foam and carpet make excellent targets or bases for your dog.

HINT: *If your dog already has foot targets mastered, then feel free to skip ahead to Chapter 3, Run the bases, on page 26. If you want to learn this paw-targeting skill or refresh your target training, come right this way.*

Let's get started

As mentioned previously, you only need one target or base to get started. Eventually, you will be adding a second, third, or fourth target. An ideal target would be 24 inches to 36 inches in diameter and square, rectangular, or circular in shape. It is best if the targets are easy for your dog to see and have a texture that is different from the main surface you are working on. If you are working on carpet, then the targets should be smooth, something like pieces of thin wood or Frisbees would work.

If working on a smooth surface, then your targets might be pieces of carpet or foam. Just be sure to secure the targets so that they don't slide around. Outside on grass, you can use either smooth or textured targets, as long as they are easy for your dog to see.

You will also need some yummy treats and a marker, either a clicker or a marker word such as "yes". A bowl or a treat pouch will make things easier, so using them is highly recommended.

Suitable targets include Frisbees, carpet remnants, or low platforms.

HINT: *From here on I will use the word "marker" to refer to either a click or a verbal marker word such as "yes". You can use either marker but stick to one type of marker per session, either a click or a word.*

Ready, set, go …

Keep your sessions short and sweet. The easiest way to keep a session short is to count out 10 treats and when the treats are gone, your session is over. You can do several sessions, but having a short break in between to re-stock treats gives both you and your dog a nice break.

I like to use a treat pouch to keep my treats close at hand. You can start with your treats in a bowl on a table but eventually, your dog will be moving around you so having treats in a pouch at your waist makes things less complicated. You can also grab 10 treats, hold them in your hand, and then feed them one at a time.

Get everything organized before you start working with your dog. Place your target on a nearby table or another surface off of the floor or ground. Be sure to practice a time or two *without* your dog, if paw targeting is new to you and your dog.

Clicker and treat bag.

If you are totally new to positive training, you can "load the marker". This is done by marking and then giving your dog a treat. The three steps are: say *yes* or click, pause a beat, then give your dog a treat. Repeat until all 10 treats are gone. Reload 10 treats and repeat. You are not marking any movement or behavior in particular. You are just teaching your dog that when they hear a marker that something good is coming. It is not necessary to load the marker, you can just start the session, if you prefer.

HINT: *To make your intentions crystal clear to your dog, always mark and then treat. If you will be reaching into a treat bag or bowl for a treat, wait until after you mark to move your hand into the container. If you are holding treats in your hand, mark and then pause a beat before tossing or handing a treat to your dog.*

Right on target

Now that you are prepared, place the target on the floor and look down at it. Be ready to mark as soon as your dog moves toward the target. Most likely your dog will be curious about this new object in their environment and will move to investigate it.

HINT: *If your dog is totally new to foot targeting, place the target just in front of you, between you and your dog. You now have the target and your body position working in your favor, drawing your dog to the target.*

It may not take your dog long to realize that the target is just a piece of carpet or plastic that isn't of much interest to them. Thus, they may lose interest in the target quickly if you don't mark and treat as they approach it. You want to mark any movement toward the target. Try to mark early so that you catch your dog moving toward the target and not away from it.

The first few foot target sessions are broken into small, simple steps so that you can see where this exercise is going. The multiple steps may look daunting, but they usually happen *very* quickly. Make sure to read through all three game plans before you start your first session so you know what to expect and how to move forward. Your dog will interact with the target in their own, unique way, so they may not follow the steps exactly as written.

ABOVE LEFT: *Start with the target directly between you and your dog.*

LEFT: *Sir starts toward me and the foot target. Note that I am looking at the target and not at Sir.*

Sir moves to foot target.

Sir is marked for stepping on the target.

Sir is fed a treat while standing on the target.

Your dog may walk over and stand on or very near the target the very first time you put it down or they may not pay any attention to it. Take what your dog gives you and jump ahead if your dog offers standing near or on the target. You are shaping your dog to go to and stand on a target, so don't get in your dog's way if they leap ahead!

Get on base

PART A

1. Get your foot target and 10 treats organized.
2. Practice without your dog if this is new to you and your dog.
3. Load the clicker (optional).
4. Place the target on the floor and look down at it.
5. Mark as your dog moves to investigate the target.
6. Give your dog a treat in place.
7. If your dog is a good distance from the target, mark as they move toward it again.
8. If your dog is on or very near the target, move and call them off the target. Give another treat when they move off the target. (If you give a treat for coming back away from the target to you, then use 20 treats per session.)
9. Move back by the target and keep marking, then treating until you have used up all of your treats.
10. Pick up your target and store it back on the table until you are ready to start your next session.

PART B

1. Get your target and treats organized.
2. Place the target on the floor and look down at it.
3. Mark as your dog approaches the target.
4. Give your dog a treat in place.
5. Keep marking, then treating as your dog moves closer to the target.
6. Mark your dog standing with one front paw on the target.
7. Mark your dog standing with both front paws on the target.
8. End the session by picking up the target when all of your treats are gone.

PART C

1. Get your props and 20 treats organized.
2. Put the target on the floor and look down at it.
3. Mark as your dog moves to the target; then treat while your dog is standing on the target.
4. Once your dog is readily going to the target and standing on it with at least one front paw, start marking and treating only when they are on the target. Then toss or feed the treat away from the target.
5. Now mark and treat only when your dog goes and stands with both front paws on the target. Then toss or feed the treat away from the target.
6. End the session by picking up the target when all of your treats are gone.

The goal is to get your dog going to and standing on the target with both front feet. Once your dog is comfortable going to the target, you will be withholding your mark until your dog places both front feet on the target. It may take more than three sessions to get to this point or your dog may get there during the very first session. Keep your sessions short and snappy and you will soon have a dog happily seeking the target. If your dog gets stalled or you get frustrated, take a long break. Then think, plan, and do another session later.

Hitting a moving target

Once your dog is going directly back to stand on the target after receiving a treat away from the target, start moving your position around the target or tossing treats to different areas around the target. You are generalizing the approach to the target so your dog learns to move to the target from any direction.

Now that your dog is seeking the target, you can move the target around the ground or floor of the area you are working in. You are generalizing your position in relation to the target. No matter where you stand or where your dog starts relative to the target, you want your dog to head to the target with enthusiasm!

HINT: *As you move your dog's starting point farther from the target, use a happy voice to encourage your dog to run to the target.*

In the beginning, keep the target fairly close to your dog so that you are quickly getting in a lot of repetitions and your dog is receiving tons of treats. Eventually, you will move the target farther from your dog such that your dog learns to go to the target from any angle and from a good distance, roughly 10 to 12 feet.

Further afield

Once your dog actively seeks the target from different angles and longer distances, you are ready to move your foot target to an entirely new location. Try a different room in your house or another part of your yard. Set your dog up for success by starting close to the target. You will soon be able to send your dog to the target from a distance.

HINT: *Don't be in a hurry to move on to the next step. Build confidence and enthusiasm for each new step as your dog learns to seek the target.*

You have been standing patiently during this training as you waited for your dog to offer to move toward the target. Now you can start adding a physical cue, a hand gesture that points to the target. Try to slip your gesture in as soon as your dog eats their treat and before they head back to the target. Ideally, you would like the hand signal to become the cue that tells your dog to go to the target, but don't get worried if your dog doesn't wait for your signal at this point.

HINT: *One measure of success in this game is having your dog run to the target when you cue them by pointing to the target.*

Easy peasy, but wait!

That's it for the first Green grass game – Get on base! Before you move on to the next game and start adding bases and obstacles between the bases, make sure your dog is enthusiastically going to the base from a good distance.

Sir running to base.

You also want your dog to follow your hand signal indicating the base. This includes having your dog wait for the signal before heading to the base. If your dog heads to the base without waiting for your hand cue, try asking your dog for a sit or down, feed several treats while they hold that position, and then indicate the base with your hand point.

HINT: *Games are fun because you play them with your dog. You are the director of traffic, telling your dog when and what to do in each game.*

Reinforcing both behaviors, the wait and getting on the base, gets your dog tuned in to you and makes you an important part of the game. You will be indicating what you want your dog to do in each of the games, so you want your dog looking to you for direction.

Let's expand this game, and make it a bit more challenging and a lot more fun for you and your dog, by getting your dog **Running the bases** in Chapter 3.

Cheat sheet #2

Run the bases

1. Fun first!
2. Practice without your dog.
3. Add a second target close to the first one.
4. Move the two targets farther apart as your dog gains confidence.
5. Optional: Add a jump or set of cavalettis between the two targets.
6. Add a third target to your setup.
7. Add a fourth target for a full set of bases.
8. Place low jumps or cavalettis between bases.

To win: Dog runs directly from base to base on cue. (Using two to four bases.)

Level up: Dog runs directly from base to base and negotiates jumps or cavalettis.

Challenge: _____

_____

CHAPTER 3

Run the bases

Getting on base is just the start. Now it is time to get your dog moving between bases. If you haven't already added a hand signal to tell your dog when to go to a base, the time has come to do so. Refer back to Chapter 2 for instructions on adding the hand cue before starting the Run the bases game.

HINT: *Start playing the games using treats and switch to toys or play with only treats or only toys. Your choice! Adapt the games to you and your dog's preferences.*

Two for the price of one
Now that you have a hand signal that gets your dog moving to a base or target with enthusiasm, it's time to add a second base. If possible, use an identical base or one that is very similar to your first base.

Start by placing the bases quite close together. You want going from one mat to the other to be a no-brainer for your dog. Plus, if the targets are close, you can get in a lot of quick repetitions in a very short amount of time. Again, you want your dog to wait for your hand signal before changing bases.

Sir goes to the second mat when I cue him with a hand signal.

Sir moving between mats.

Feet in motion

Let's look at adding a second target in more detail. Place one target on the ground near you. Mark, then give a treat to your dog for going to and standing on it. Walk a few steps away and place the second target on the floor. Don't go very far, a few feet is plenty. You will be standing between the two targets but off to the side a bit. You want to stay close, but not in the path your dog will take as they move between targets.

Look and point at the second target. When your dog makes any move toward the second target, mark, then feed a treat while your dog stands on the second target. Your dog will eat their treat while standing on the second target.

Now, turn back toward the first target and point at it. When your dog makes any move back toward the first target, mark, then feed over the first target. Your dog will eat their treat while standing back on the first target. Repeat having your dog transition from one target to the other until they are moving with enthusiasm between the targets when cued.

Set up of two targets a bit farther apart.

Feeding while Sir is on the target.

Yay! Your dog has completed several round trips from target to target and back home again. I think you know where this is going, no?

Running to and fro

When your dog is happily moving from target to target when cued, you can start moving the targets farther away from each other. Start slowly, just a foot at a time, and then a bit farther as your dog shows how brilliant they are.

Eventually, you want to get your dog moving at a faster pace by upping your enthusiasm. You can do this by verbally encouraging your dog to trot or run to the next target with a high-pitched, happy voice. If happily saying "Let's go!" doesn't get your dog moving faster, try trotting or running with them a few times as they go from one target to the other.

If your dog is into tugs or toys, you can mark when your dog gets on the next target and then throw your tug or ball for your dog to bring back to you. Just be sure to wait for your dog to stop on the target before marking, then throw your tug, toy, or treat.

HINT: *If you plan to toss treats, make sure they are large and easily seen by your dog. Otherwise, your dog may spend a lot of time hunting for them.*

Take a leap

You can now add an obstacle such as a jump or set of cavalettis between the bases. **Cavalettis** are very low jump-type obstacles that are usually used in sets of 4 to 6.

 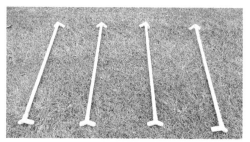

Various types of cavalettis.   *A set of cavalettis ready for use.*

HINT: *For most dogs, the distance between cavalettis should be the shoulder height of the dog and the poles of the cavalettis should be raised above the ground at about wrist height of the dog.*

Adjust the distance between the cavalettis such that your dog can easily trot over them without hitting them. You may also need to adjust the height of the cavalettis for your dog.

HINT: *Be sure to adjust the distance between cavalettis such that your dog can easily trot over them without hitting a bar.*

If adding cavalettis, you first want your dog trotting between the bases. You can then add one cavaletti at a time, on the path your dog is taking, until your entire set of cavalettis has been added. If your dog has never been introduced to cavalettis, practice without the bases in the picture, as explained below. Once your dog is comfortable trotting over your set of cavalettis, add them between the two bases.

HINT: *Always introduce a new behavior or prop, such as a jump or target, away from the game. Once your dog is proficient and confident in performing the new action, then add it to your game.*

Remember that these are your games so every game and every addition to a game is optional. Design the games to fit you and your dog. You can always add new elements to games as your and your dog's skills and confidence increase. Low jumps and sets of cavalettis make great obstacles to add between bases.

To add a set of cavalettis between two bases, start by setting up one cavaletti with no bases present.

Teaching cavaletti work

1. To get your dog trotting over one cavalettis, start by having your dog sit a short distance in front of the cavaletti.
2. Then leave your dog sitting and move to the other side of the cavaletti.
3. Call your dog to you.
4. If your dog avoids the cavaletti, you can lure your dog over the cavaletti with a tasty treat.
5. Hold a treat in your hand and lure your dog over the cavaletti by walking beside the cavaletti while your hand and dog pass over it.
6. Once your dog has walked over the cavaletti, you will feed the treat.

7. Have your dog sit and face the cavaletti again.
8. Now lure your dog to walk back over the cavaletti to their starting point.
9. Repeat once more while still holding a treat in your hand.
10. Now repeat the process while holding your hand just as you did with the treat, but *without* a treat in your hand. (You will no longer hold a treat in your hand for the remainder of this exercise.)

11. Encourage your dog to trot over the cavaletti by trotting alongside your dog, then mark and feed a treat on the other side of the cavaletti.
12. When your dog is trotting freely over the cavaletti, add another cavaletti.
13. Continue adding cavalettis until your dog is trotting over the entire set in both directions.

Only lure your dog over the cavaletti(s) a few times. The lure gives your dog the idea of what you want them to do and encourages them to follow your hand as a cue or physical signal.

HINT: *Luring helps your dog understand what you are asking them to do or where you want them to go. Lure sparingly, three times is plenty!*

Adding a jump

If your dog is familiar with jumping, you can add a jump directly between the bases. If your dog is new to jumping, start with a low jump and see the directions below. To add a jump between bases, follow the steps below. Repeat each step until your dog is confidently running from base to base before moving to the next step.

Adding a jump between bases

1. Get your dog running between two bases or foot targets when cued by your hand signal.
2. Place only the jump standards or objects, such as upside-down bowls, in the path between the bases or targets. (Your dog will be running between the jump standards or bowls.)
3. Move to the next step when your dog is again running between the bases.

---

4. Place the jump bar on the ground between or next to the jump standards.
5. Raise the jump bar to the lowest level.
6. Raise the jump bar to the next higher level until it is at the level you desire.

Sir freely moving from base to base.

Sir running between bowls with no jump bar.

Now the jump bar has been added but is on the ground.

Finally, Sir is jumping a low jump while running between the bases.

The goal of adding obstacles between the bases is not to have your dog jumping high jumps or negotiating cavalettis, but to spice up the game for your dog!

Running all of the bases

The last step is to add more targets or bases to your setup. After your dog is used to moving between two targets, you can add a third target in a triangular pattern and direct your dog to either of the vacant targets by standing in the middle of the targets and pointing at the target you want your dog to go to.

Next, add a fourth target in a square or diamond pattern. Now your dog can run around the bases, stopping at each target, while you stand in the center of the setup. You can then send your dog forward around the bases in the same direction or back the way they came.

HINT: *At this point, stand in the center of your setup and send your dog around the perimeter and not through the center.*

Sir moving around three bases or target mats.

Sir running (or trotting) the bases!

Start slowly, with your dog walking or trotting between bases. Then ramp up the speed to a canter between bases that are a good distance apart.

Your body position is key as you direct your dog around the bases. You should face the direction you want your dog to go and hold your arm out toward them. Later, you can add verbal directional cues, if you desire.

HINT: *You can either pull or push your dog, depending on which arm you use to direct your dog. Try using each arm and see which one works best for you and your dog.*

Once you decide which arm to use to cue your dog to move from base to base, you can easily remember your choice by keying on if you are pulling or pushing your dog around your setup. The use of either arm is fine, just remember to be consistent from game to game so that neither you nor your dog gets confused.

Lifelines

If you get stuck introducing the **Running the bases** game, here are a few lifelines to help:

- **Dog doesn't stop on target** – Try slowing down your dog as they approach the target by indicating the target with a slower arm sweep or by walking slower if you are moving between the bases beside your dog.
- **Dog doesn't stop on target** – Reduce the level of your verbal enthusiasm to encourage your dog to move more slowly and thoughtfully.
- **Dog doesn't stop on target** – If you are using a large triangular or diamond-shaped setup, try shrinking your setup so your dog doesn't get moving fast.

Ramp up your dog's speed again, once your dog is consistently stopping on each target before being sent on to the next base. Eventually, you want your dog moving at the pace that you feel is appropriate. For most dogs, cantering or trotting would be ideal, but the speed can be adjusted to suit your dog's needs and the obstacles your dog will be negotiating between bases.

Congratulations!

You and your dog have completed the second enrichment game, **Run the bases**. This simple game is a fun way to get your dog thinking while moving. Mindless running is not possible nor desired while playing enrichment games. You want your dog hooked up to you as you direct them through each game.

One way to keep your dog on their toes is by adding a pause or cueing a behavior such as sit or down before you send them on to the next base. Your dog has to look to you to know when to move and which base to target. The ability to direct your dog around your setup is what makes these games interesting and fun! You stay connected with your dog and your dog stays connected to you.

HINT: *If your dog starts to anticipate moving around the bases in one direction, send them back in the opposite direction.*

Now that we have your dog moving, let's look at the other equipment you will need to play other enrichment games. Don't worry, all of the necessary items are inexpensive or can be made from items you probably already own.

Onward!

Cheat sheet

Game gear

1. Clicker or another marker
2. Treats and a pouch or bowl
3. Toys: balls or tugs (a tug can be made by tying a knot in a heavy sock)
4. Flirt pole – (optional)
5. Cones (8 to 12) or other types of individual markers or plastic 3-inch tape and stakes to hold the tape off of the ground
6. Foot targets (3 or 4)
7. X-pen (exercise pen) or another see-through barrier
8. Play area (indoor or outside)
9. Jumps, platforms, etc

CHAPTER 4

Play ball or flirt?

Fortunately, not a lot of equipment is needed to play enrichment games. Most of the necessary supplies can be found around your home or purchased at a minimal cost. Be creative. I will offer homemade ideas that work well and suggest buying only a piece or two of equipment that is far superior to its homemade counterpart.

Gear needed

To play individual games, certain items are necessary. A list of equipment needed for each game is provided, allowing you to gather the required items before starting to play.

Gear such as a clicker, treats and a pouch, tugs, a flirt pole, cones or other ground markers, plastic tape and stakes, foot targets, and a see-through barrier will be used. You may also want to gather bowls and PVC pipe or other materials for low jumps. A pen to jot notes in this book will also come in handy as you play.

Much of the gear can be improvised such as making a tug out of an old sock or braided fleece. The only piece of equipment I suggest buying is a flirt pole with a flexible handle. Having two flirt poles, a small and a large one, allows for indoor and outdoor play.

Sir as a pup with a couple of homemade fleece tugs.

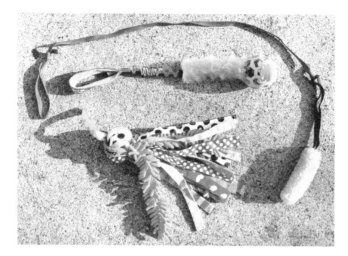

There are a plethora of colorful tugs available. I prefer those with bungee handles.

Flirt poles usually come in either short or long sizes. Long flirt poles are often made of a horse lunge whip with a toy attached.

HINT: *A flirt pole is a flexible rod with a handle at one end and a heavy string attached to the other. A toy that can be used as a tug is attached to the end of the string.*

Flirt poles can be made using a broom handle, cord, and toy but these are not ideal. Instead, I suggest you purchase a flirt pole with a flexible rod because it is much easier on your arms and shoulders. The small flirt pole I use is pictured above. If you do purchase a flirt pole, be sure to get one that has a flexible pole rather than a rigid one.

Cones and other markers

If you use cones as markers, I suggest using flexible 12-inch cones for safety. Orange traffic cones are perfect. You can also use other types of markers. Think of tall plastic containers with lids such as cottage cheese containers or upside-down plastic bowls. See what you find around your house before you purchase cones.

Buckets can be alternate markers.

If you prefer, you can use plastic non-adhesive tape to mark out your playing field in the more advanced games. This 3-inch tape can be found in many stores that sell building materials. It often comes with "caution" or "danger" lettering.

An example of "caution" tape that is useful to demarcate the play area.

If you plan to use plastic tape, you will also need some stakes to hold the tape off of the ground. The height of the tape will depend on your dog's height. You want the tape to be at about the level of your dog's elbows. I use some kabob skewers that I don't use for cooking anymore. They can easily be stuck in the ground and have a rounded eye at the other end.

Kabob skewers for holding up marking tape.

See-through barrier

You will need a barrier when you get to the Cone squares game. I find an X-pen (exercise pen) works well, but don't buy one if you don't have one. You will only use the barrier for a short time, so rather look for an alternative prop.

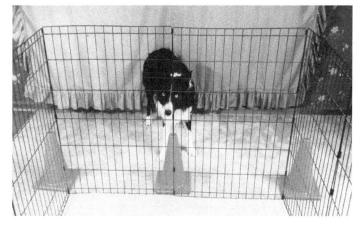

An X-pen used as a see-through barrier.

Your dog should be able to see through the barrier but not go through it. It is just a prop to help your dog be successful by eliminating an incorrect choice. The barrier should be lightweight and stable for maximum safety.

What you use as a barrier will depend upon the type of marker you are using: cones or bowls versus heavy string or plastic tape. So wait until you need a barrier to worry about getting your choice of barrier finalized. If you use plastic tape to mark off your play area, you may be able to use the tape as a barrier.

Play area

All that's left for you to figure out is where to play the games. If you have a room with a large open area, I suggest you start to play there. Just be sure the floor is not slick as you don't want your dog slipping as they play. You also need to make sure that you have at least 4 feet of clearance around the entire perimeter of your setup. You definitely don't want your dog running into any furniture or walls during play.

My inside play area.

HINT: *Always keep safety uppermost in your mind as you play.*

A fenced outside area is ideal as long as it has good footing and is free from obstacles that your dog might run into. Be aware of trees, chairs, or other obstructions that your dog could crash into. Often your dog will be looking at you and moving at speed so give them room to swing wide around your marker cones or tape without having to worry about running into anything.

One of my outside fenced play areas.

As you pull together your game gear remember that, eventually, your dog will probably be moving at speed as they play. Safety first! Keep equipment decisions based on safety rather than on how colorful or eye-catching your setup is.

You can always upgrade elements of your play area and gear over time. Who doesn't like to look forward to making or purchasing a special toy or treat for their dog?

Cheat sheet

Your superpower!

1. Put fun as your top priority.
2. Practice without your dog if you aren't confident of what you are asking your dog to do. (Not really a rule but it should be.)
3. Use the same hand signals and body movements in all of the games so that your dog can predict what you want them to do.
4. Take a "snapshot" of the action you want your dog to perform by marking it.
5. Use consistent timing to mark, then reinforce by giving a treat or tossing a toy.
6. Present your treat or toy at the time and place that is most likely to set your dog up for their next move in the game.

7. Make it worthwhile for your dog to play your silly game by being generous with treats or other reinforcement such as tugging, flirt pole play, or ball tossing.

CHAPTER 5

Your superpower!

Playing with your dog is your superpower! Are there any other animals who enjoy playing with us as much as our dogs do? How fortunate we are to be able to engage with our dogs in fun games, games that enrich our and their lives and build lasting bonds.

Most dogs are driven to chase, catch, and control prey. You can channel that instinctive drive into games that build your relationship while you play together. Your dog may love to tug, chase a Frisbee or ball, or just play silly games with you.

As you dive into enrichment games, you will find that simple games build into more complex ones. Thus, the games are structured to be played in order. You and your dog will use the skills learned in previous games to play more advanced

Play can be simple but amazingly powerful!

games. If you already have the required skills in place, I still encourage you to play a short game session of the current game before moving on to the next game.

So what is structured play? It is playing a game with rules that form a framework. It is this framework that provides clarity for you and your dog. A system of best practices, if you will, that define the key elements of all of the games. Let me clarify.

Games rule

All games have rules so that you know how to play them. The following general rules facilitate clear communication between you and your dog, and are used in all the enrichment games. Specific rules, and step-by-step instructions, are provided for each game.

Let's look at best practices for playing enrichment games:
1. Fun is priority one!
2. Practice with an imaginary dog when you are not sure what to do.
3. Use the same physical and verbal cues in all of the games.
4. Define and look for a specific slice of behavior to mark.
5. Mark, *then* reinforce. Allow a short pause between marking or clicking and delivering the treat or tug
6. Use the delivery of your reinforcer to set your dog up for their next move in the game.
7. Make it worthwhile for your dog to play your silly game. Be generous!

These basic rules form the foundational structure for enrichment games. The rules or best practices are not meant to limit you but to set you and your dog up for quick success playing the games. Clear communication with your dog makes them more relaxed, confident, and happy.

Me and Sir having fun together!

Fun is the priority – Rule #1

The first rule when playing enrichment games is to have fun. A game without fun isn't really a game, it's just a chore and everyone already has enough of those. If you find yourself or your dog getting frustrated or confused along the way, stop and take a break.

Even if things are going swimmingly, a break provides a good time to chill with your dog and get some "us" time in. High-energy dogs love action, but too much continuous activity can ramp up your dog's arousal beyond the optimal level.

Sometimes during a break, you will have a lightbulb moment and instantly see a more fun way to play the game or realize how to get over the sticking point that has been bothering you. Or maybe during a break, you will ponder just how great it feels to spend time just being with your dog.

Practice with an imaginary dog – Rule #2

Your dog will thank you for practicing a new game without them. Yes, really! Of course, you want to include your dog as much as possible as you play the games. The rub is that when you start playing a game, you may not be sure what you want your dog to do, where you should be stationed, or how to incorporate a new element into the game.

When you do a quick run-through without your dog, you are setting yourself and your dog up for success. It is a win-win situation. Your practice boosts your confidence and allows your dog to relax and happily engage with you.

Practicing without your dog is a win-win.

Directing traffic – Rule #3

To begin, you will be using hand signals and body position to communicate with your dog as you play the games. These are non-verbal cues. If you use a word as a mark, the word is a verbal cue telling your dog that a treat or toy is now available to them. Eventually, you will also be adding verbal cues to the games.

Whether you use words or body movements to "talk" to your dog, you want your communication to be clear. If your dog doesn't understand what you are asking them to do, there is no way they will be able to answer with the correct response. Most likely your dog will try to please you by offering a guess at what you want.

If your dog guesses correctly, all good and well, but it is still a guess. You can't count on your dog being a better guesser than you are a coach. Guessing leads to mistakes and mistakes lead to frustration for both you and your dog.

Paying attention to your words and movements makes your conversation clear and precise. You know exactly what you are asking of your dog and your dog understands how they are to respond. With practice, the conversation between you and your dog becomes like a dance, simple yet elegant.

HINT: *A good cue asks for only one action from your dog, and only that action. To be clear, your hand signal or body position must be consistent, as seen by your dog.*

Mark to capture – Rule #4

The purpose of marking an action is to tell your dog what movement you want them to repeat. Just like us, dogs do what they find reinforcing. If you mark, then treat your dog for bowing, they will offer to bow more often. The key to success is capturing the exact snapshot of the moment or action that you want your dog to give you more of.

To get the precise freeze frame of your dog in motion, you need to first see the moment and then mark that moment. Catching a precise moment requires that you know what you are looking for, can observe it, and are ready to mark it. Anticipation is key to catching a slice of behavior. Simple but not easy.

HINT: *Look for the movement that predicts the moment you want to mark. If you wait to see the exact moment you want to capture, you will be late marking it.*

Seeing a specific moment requires keen observation of your dog. You are looking for just that one slice of action. Think of it as one frame of an old film reel, if you are old enough to remember movies on film.

Each slice of behavior can be seen as a single frame or snapshot of that behavior.

Even a simple behavior has multiple mark or click points. Each slice of behavior happens fast!

Often, the behavior you want to mark will be over before you capture it with a click or verbal marker.

There are many possible images on the film to choose from, but only one is the exact moment you want to capture. You don't have to be quite this precise because, lucky for you, your dog is forgiving and will help you out. Just get as close as you can to marking what you want.

HINT: *If you don't know exactly what you intend to mark, there is no way you will know when to click or say yes.*

Mark, then reinforce – Rule #5

How you handle marking and delivering your treat or toy makes a huge difference when playing with your dog. If you click and move your hand to get a treat at the same time, your dog will notice the movement of your hand toward your pouch or bowl and ignore the click. Likewise, if you throw your toy while saying yes, your dog will key on the movement of the hand throwing the toy and not on your marker word.

HINT: *Your body movements are much more salient or noticeable to your dog than clicks or words are.*

The first time I point to the target, Sir looks at my hand to make sure I am not moving it toward my treat pouch.

Because I kept my hand pointed at the target during the first trial, on the second trial Sir went to the target without glancing at my hand.

Consistency in timing and reinforcement equals clarity for your dog. Marking and starting to reinforce your dog simultaneously means that your dog learns to watch you closely, waiting for any telltale movement that a treat or toy is going to be delivered.

If your dog focuses on watching you, they are paying less attention to where they are going. As enrichment games get more advanced, you will want your dog to pay attention to where they are going as there will be cones, targets, and other equipment for them to negotiate at speed.

I present to you – Rule #6

Now let's look at the delivery of your treat or toy. Where you deliver your reinforcer is almost as important as marking the moment you want to be repeated. It is always a good idea to plan where you will present your treat or toy before you start playing. If you practice without your dog, don't forget to include the presentation of the treat or toy. This is another important key to game success.

You want to place your reinforcer so that:
• You encourage your dog to seek a target.
• You move your dog on to the next step in the game.
• You set your dog up to start the game again.

During the games, I will suggest where and how to place your treat or toy. Sometimes you will hand the reinforcer to your dog, sometimes toss it, and sometimes just drop it.

Treat delivery all depends on what you want your dog to do next. You are marking the action you want more of and your treat delivery sets your dog up to give you more of that action. Another win-win situation.

Generous to a fault – Rule #7

Finally, your dog won't know how much fun these games are until they learn to play them well. At first, they won't be sure what is going on since the games will be a

new experience for them. To keep your dog in the game until they learn to love the game, you need to be super generous with your treats and toys.

Tons of different treats are available. Be generous!

HINT: *Playing the games will become self-reinforcing for your dog. Eventually, you will be able to cut back on your use of treats and toys.*

Think about how challenging it was to learn a fun game that you now play effortlessly. No matter how much fun it was to watch others play the game, there was probably a learning curve that you had to master to really enjoy playing it.

The same goes for your dog. Keep their interest and enthusiasm high as they learn the games by generously showering your dog with toys, treats, and happy encouragement along the way.

Barb offering a treat to Gold.

Play is your superpower!

Games are the secret sauce that adds spice and variety to your and your dog's lives. It's time to replace your old boring routines with some new exciting games. Is your dog ready to add some secret sauce to their life?

Is your dog distracted?
It's time to get engaged ...

Cheat sheet #3

Distraction action

1. Fun first!
2. Gather smelly treats or a favorite toy.
3. Start in a familiar place – ask your dog to sit.
4. If your dog is successful, hold the treat or toy within inches of your dog's nose and cue sit.
5. When your dog is successful, move on to the next step, but when your dog struggles, break the step down until it is easy for your dog.
6. Continue to increase the difficulty for your dog as you move through the steps.

To win: Dog sits on cue while you quickly wave a treat or toy near their nose.

Level up: Dog sits on cue while you wave, bounce, or sing in an unfamiliar location.

Challenge: _____

_____

CHAPTER 6

Distraction action

Distraction is the name, but fun is the aim of this game! Please commit to making all enrichment games fun for you and your dog. A game isn't a game at all if it isn't fun. If you are not laughing every time you play one of the games in this book, then you really are missing out on the best part of enrichment games – the fun of playing with your dog as you build an amazing relationship.

The Distraction action game may be familiar to you, but it usually isn't framed as a light-hearted game. We are about to change that!

This game, as presented here, is easy to play and has a simple goal – for your dog to listen to a cue and perform a familiar action. The catch is that you will be adding distracting elements to the game, one at a time.

HINT: *Let's look at the example below to see if you and your dog are already pros at this game. If this game is easy-peasy for your dog, feel free to skip ahead to the* Engagement *game on page 61.*

The example of this game will feature the sit behavior since most dogs are proficient at sitting when asked. If your dog is more experienced with down, go ahead and substitute down in this game. "Proficient" means that your dog responds quickly and correctly when cued once. When you say "sit", your dog should sit immediately and not lie down or bow. Just remember to keep things fun for you and your dog!

Distraction action

The object of this game is to determine just how proficient your dog is at performing an easy, well-known behavior. Start the game in an area where your dog is comfortable and ask for a sit. If your dog quickly complies, then move on to the next level of the game. If your dog doesn't sit quickly, then work on sitting until your dog is quickly and confidently sitting when cued. Customize the following list of distractions to suit you, your dog, and your play area.

Here are the levels of the Distraction action game, using *sit* as the target behavior.

Sit when asked

1. In a quiet familiar room.
2. In a quiet familiar room while you hold a high-value treat or a favorite toy just *inches* from your dog's nose.
3. While you *slowly* wave a high-value treat or a favorite toy just inches from your dog's nose.
4. While you *quickly* wave a high-value treat or a favorite toy just inches from your dog's nose.

---

5. While you are turned sideways to your dog.
6. While you have your back to your dog.
7. While you face your dog and wave one arm.
8. While you wave both arms.
9. While you jump up and down.
10. While you sing a song.
11. While a favorite toy or food is placed nearby.
12. While you …

Sir sitting with a tug held near his head.

The list can be extended as far as you want to go. Once you have completed your personal list of challenges, go back and run through the list again in an unfamiliar room and then outside.

The point of this game is to see what your dog is capable of and to grow their capabilities. Do they know the sit as well as you thought they did? How about their down? Or stand? Or bow? Having a few strong verbally cued behaviors will be essential as you and your dog move on to the next game, the Engagement game.

Sir sitting while I twirl the tug.

Along the way, you may find that your dog needs more than one cue, sits very slowly, or waits several seconds before starting to sit. If your dog struggles on a step, then you have a normal dog. You just need to focus on that level until your dog is performing with confidence.

Let's break it down

A great way to help your dog be successful is to break down each level into smaller steps. Step 2 is a good step to use as an example because a lot of dogs struggle to sit with a treat or toy only inches from their nose. Let's break that level down when using a treat (but you can substitute a favorite tug or toy for the treat).

Your dog sits readily when asked with virtually no distractions, but with a smelly treat nearby, all bets are off. Breaking down that step into smaller pieces is the solution.

HINT: *This break-it-down technique can be used for any level of any game.*

The goal is to make the troublesome step simple enough for your dog to be successful. Keep breaking the level down into smaller steps until your dog can perform the step quickly and easily. Then slowly increase the difficulty until you are successfully back at the step where you started.

As you remember, step 2 is: *Hold a treat inches from your dog's nose and ask for a sit.*

Possible breakdown of step 2 treat position:
1. Treat behind your back.
2. Treat at your side.
3. Treat halfway to your dog's nose.
4. Treat a few inches from your dog's nose.

If necessary, break these steps down even further. Maybe start with a piece of kibble instead of a smelly treat or stand a few steps farther away from your dog so that the treat is not quite so alluring. Or move the treat only an inch or two closer to your dog's nose between cues to make it easier for your dog to succeed.

 HINT: *Remember that you can help your dog to become proficient at each mini-step along the way by repeating the step several times over a few sessions.*

Sir sitting while I lift my leg.

 HINT: *As your dog learns this game, they usually begin to move through the steps more quickly.*

Sir sitting while I jump up and down.

Set the levels of this game up to suit your and your dog's needs. You may be surprised at how well your dog does on some advanced levels and which steps trip them up.

How did it go?

Did you and your dog find this game easy, fun, or challenging? The purpose of this game is to set you and your dog up for success playing the following games. If you have mastered this game, then you are ready for the added challenge of the Engagement game.

Now you can go back through the steps using a different cue. If you started with *sit*, you could work on *down*. Each time through, the steps will be easier for your dog. Play this game with as few or as many cues as you want.

After you have done *sit* and *down* you could switch randomly between the cues to keep your dog on their toes.

In the next game, not only will you be getting your dog in motion, but you will also be having them focus on a target, either a treat or a toy. The tricky part is that they will be focused on that target while you ask them to sit or down.

If your dog successfully performs the cued behavior, they are then released to the target. It may sound confusing, but you will soon learn how to lead your dog through all of the levels of the game, one step at a time.

Cheat sheet #4

Engagement game

1. Start this game by placing a tug between you and your dog.
2. Release your dog to get the toy and tug.
3. Reset your dog. This time release your dog and immediately ask your dog to sit.
4. If your dog sits successfully, release them to get the toy and tug.
5. If your dog keeps moving to the toy, pull it quickly back to you before your dog grabs it.
6. As your dog is successful, move to the side and then back to stand by your dog.

To win: Dog sits on cue after released but before they get to the toy.

Level up: Dog retrieves tug back to you after released to get it.

Challenge: _____

CHAPTER 7

Let's get engaged

Are you ready to ramp up the challenge for you and your dog? The Engagement game takes your dog to an amazing level of self-control. This is a simple game that will impress your friends and family. Who doesn't love that? It's not a terribly difficult game for your dog to excel at if it is broken down into small bite-sized steps. Fortunately, you are now an expert at breaking steps into mini-steps!

Before you jump into the game, you need to understand how engagement is different from distraction. As you know, distraction is all about your dog paying attention to you, no matter what you do or what goes on around them. Engagement is similar in that you want your dog listening to you, but now they will be focused on a treat or toy away from you, instead of focusing on you.

HINT: *Let's compare and contrast these two games.*

- **Distraction game** = Dog *listens to you* while ignoring everything in the environment.
- **Engagement game** = Dog *listens to you* while focusing on something in the environment.

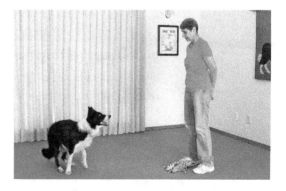

Sir sitting while being distracted. (Sir is focused on me.)

*Sir sitting while being engaged.
(Sir is focused on the tug.)*

Since you have already played Distraction action, you know what distractions are all about. In this game, your dog is going to build amazing self-control while you both have fun. Laughing is a required element of this game! Can your dog focus on a yummy treat or favorite toy and still respond to you? You are soon going to find out.

On the level

There are three levels to the Engagement game – Intro, Intermediate, and Advanced. Before you start, I suggest you read through all three levels and decide where you and your dog should begin. If in doubt, start with the level that you are confident your dog will nail and move through that level quickly. That success will set you and your dog up for continued success at the next level.

Obviously, the Intro level is the place to start if this is all new to you and your dog, so let's start there.

Treat, tug, or ball?

Since you will be placing your treat or toy target on the floor, I suggest you start playing this game while sitting on a cushion on the floor.

You can start out using a treat or a toy, but I suggest you begin this game by using treats. Treats are small and easier to cover

The game setup is: sitting on a cushion with the tug on the floor between me and Sir.

with your hand than a tug or ball would be. Unless your dog has played a game similar to this one, you are probably going to have to cover your target treat a few times to prevent your dog from stealing it right out from under your nose.

Get set … play!

All that you need to start the Intro level of this game are some treats and a cushion. You can skip the cushion if you prefer to sit on the floor, but you want to be comfortable while you play. Keep a stash of treats nearby but inaccessible to your dog. A covered bowl or container works fine.

Engagement game – *intro level*

1. Get 10 treats ready and set other treats aside in a covered container.
2. Sit on a cushion on the floor.
3. Practice *without* your dog, if this is a new game for you and your dog.
4. Your dog will be standing or sitting directly in front of you, close enough that you could pet them, but not nose to nose with you.

5. Place the target treat (or small toy) on the floor just in front of you and look down at it.
6. If your dog moves forward to get the treat, quickly cover it with your hand, then reset your dog a little farther away from you and begin again.
7. If your dog holds position, mark with a word or click, pick up the treat, and feed it to your dog. Your dog will have remained stationary the entire time.
8. Repeat placing and feeding your treats until all 10 treats have been fed.
9. End the game!

Be prepared to quickly cover the treat if your dog moves forward to get it. You want all the reinforcement to come directly from you and not from the environment. It should only take a few times of covering the treat for your dog to pause before moving to grab it. Take advantage of that pause, while your dog is thinking, to mark (say *yes*), pick up the treat, and give it to your dog.

HINT: *Play this game as many times as necessary until you are confident that your dog will hold their position until you mark and then pick up the treat and give it to them.*

If your dog is into toys, play the Intro level again using a toy. Any toy your dog goes crazy for will work. Your dog will already know this game so they should quickly adapt to a toy being used in place of a treat. Again, play this game until your dog is confident and happy. Playing this game until your dog is proficient is money in the bank and sets your dog up for success on the next level. At this point, you use either a toy or treats to reinforce your dog, not both at the same time. Start and work through the games with one reinforcer at a time, treats first and then a toy or a toy first and then treats.

Engagement game – *intermediate level*

PART A

1. Get 10 treats ready or pull out a favorite tug.
2. If using a tug, you will need to limit the length of playing tug as reinforcement to 10 seconds for each session.
3. If using treats, play the game until all 10 treats have been fed to your dog.
4. Sit on a cushion on the floor.

---

5. Your dog will be standing or sitting directly in front of you but at a fair distance, about 12 feet away.
6. Place the target (treat or toy) on the floor in front of you and look down at it.
7. Give a release cue such as *get it* and allow your dog to get the treat or toy. If using a tug, then do a super short tug session.

PART B

1. Reset your dog to their original position, place the target on the floor and release your dog to the target.
2. As soon as your dog starts toward the target, give your sit or down cue.
3. If your dog keeps moving toward the target, quickly cover it with your hand, then reset your dog a little farther away from you and begin again.
4. If your dog sits or downs as cued, mark with a word or click and release your dog to get the treat or toy. (At this level, your dog will be picking up the treat or tug from the floor.)
5. Play this game until your dog will confidently sit or down when cued before being released to the reinforcer, the treat or tug.

You can grow this game in several ways, such as allowing your dog to get close to the target before cueing a behavior. Over several sessions, allow your dog to get right up to the target before cueing a sit or down. Another alternative is to ask your dog for two or three behaviors before releasing them to the target. A typical rep might be: *Get it, sit, down, stand, get it*. Vary the number of behaviors you ask for before you release your dog to get the target, from none to three.

HINT: *To keep your dog enthused about going to the target, often allow them direct access to it, no sits or downs, once you initially release them to it. You want your dog moving quickly toward the target treat or tug.*

If you ask your dog to perform a behavior every time they move toward the reinforcer, they will start anticipating the cue and will become quite slow as they head to the target. Playing this game with speed is key to maintaining your dog's enthusiasm for it, so release your dog often and allow them to go directly to claim the target treat or tug, with no cues given to stop them.

HINT: *Don't expect your dog to run to get the target at this level of the game, but eventually, you do want your dog to run out to the target and then back to you.*

If you stop your dog and ask for a sit or down as they head to the target, be sure to release them from the cued behavior with a second release cue. Your dog would start in a stand, sit, or down and about 12 feet from you.

The cue sequence would be:
1. *Get it* – dog moves toward the target.
2. *Sit* – dog sits.
3. *Yes* or click – dog hears mark but remains sitting.
4. *Get it* – dog grabs the target.

Sir moves toward the tug.

Sir is cued to sit.

Sir sits.

Sir is released to the tug.

Moving right along

The advanced level of this game is where you get to really ramp up the fun and excitement. You will also be building amazing self-control in your dog while you both have fun, another win-win for relationship building. You can start the final level of this game inside, but you may want to take it outside so that your dog has room to run.

When you move outside, do a quick refresher with your dog. Play the first two levels of this game again to set your dog up for a successful transition to a new environment. I suggest using a fenced area for safety.

Also, once you move outside, it is much easier to use a tug or toy as your reinforcer. Treats can be difficult for you to throw and they are often difficult for your dog to find in grass.

This game level is essentially the same as the Intermediate level except that the toy will no longer be between you and your dog. Instead, you will throw the toy away from you while your dog remains stationary. You will then release your dog to the toy and sometimes allow them to get the toy and other times ask for a cued behavior or two before releasing them to the toy.

As you have probably guessed, here is where a retrieve becomes very handy. If your dog won't retrieve a toy back to you, you can attach a light line to your toy so that your dog cannot run off with it. You can then reel in the tug and your dog. Another option, if your dog will tug but won't retrieve, is to use a flirt pole.

HINT: *If you are not familiar with using a flirt pole, jump ahead to Chapter 10 for instructions on how to safely use a flirt pole in your games.*

Flirt poles are one of my very favorite pieces of equipment for playing enrichment games. If you have a dog that is into prey, they usually see the toy on the end of the flirt pole string as a squirrel. You can make the squirrel dance and run, to get your dog super engaged in the games.

HINT: *In the advanced level of this game you will have the option to pull the tug away from your dog, if they don't respond to your sit cue and instead move to grab the tug.*

NOTE: *If you have to pull the tug away from your dog twice, you need to go back and work the intermediate level again.*

Engagement game – *advanced level*

PART A

1. Use a favorite tug with a light string attached to it.
2. Place the tug on the ground.
3. Walk with your dog to a point about 12 feet away from the tug and leave your dog.
4. Now walk back to the tug, but off to the side, and pick up the string attached to the tug.
5. Release your dog to get the tug.
6. Do a short tug session when your dog brings the tug back to you.

PART B

1. Reset your dog and the tug. You will be off to the side holding the string.
2. Release your dog to the tug, but cue a sit *as soon as your dog starts moving* toward the tug.
3. If your dog keeps moving toward the tug, immediately yank the tug to you so that your dog cannot get it. Reset your dog farther away from the tug and begin again.
4. If your dog sits or downs as cued, mark with a word or click and release your dog to retrieve the tug.
5. Play for a short time and take a break.

PART C

1. When your dog is taking your cues confidently, slowly move your position back toward your dog until you are standing next to your dog.
2. Repeat Part B in your new position, standing next to your dog.

PART D

1. When your dog is confidently moving and taking all cues, then start tossing the tug instead of walking over and placing it on the ground.
2. Play short sessions often to increase success.

Sir heading to the tug which is tied to a string.

If Sir doesn't sit when cued, the tug is pulled away.

The tug flies back into my hand to prevent Sir from grabbing the tug.

Lifelines

- **Dog moves to get the tug before cued** – If your dog self-reinforces by ignoring your sit or down cue and grabs the tug, try adding a light string to the tug or use a flirt pole for this game. When your dog fails to sit or down when cued, quickly pull the tug/toy back to you before your dog can grab it.
- **Dog doesn't retrieve** – If your dog doesn't know how to retrieve, use a flirt pole in place of a tug.

Sir heading to the tug in the final level of the Engagement game.

Sir sits when cued.

Sir is released to the tug.

Sir brings the tug back for a game of tug.

If you want to teach your dog to retrieve, a step-by-step method that I have been successful with is outlined below. Note that this method will only work if your dog is already good at tugging.

HINT: *To get your dog interested in grabbing a tug toy, tie a string to it and drag it away from your dog. Most dogs cannot resist grabbing escaping prey or a tug that is moving away from them.*

Sir chasing the tug on a string.

HINT: *If your dog tugs but resists releasing the tug, check out some extra step-by-step instructions for teaching the tug release below.*

For this training, you will need a tug and some very yummy treats. A good location to start teaching the retrieve is in a very small area such as a bathroom or hallway. You want your dog quite close to you, no farther than an arm's length away to start.

The retrieve and release in four parts – *bonus*!

PART A

1. Grab your dog's favorite tug.
2. Get your dog tugging with you after cueing *get it* or another verbal cue.
3. Stop tugging and let your dog hold the tug in their mouth.
4. Offer your dog a tasty treat and wait. (Be patient.)
5. When your dog drops the tug to take the offered treat, mark and give your dog the treat.
6. Repeat (and repeat) until your dog is quickly dropping the tug when the treat is presented.

---

7. Add a release cue, such as *mine*, **before** you offer the treat.
8. When your dog is dropping the tug when you cue *mine* and before you offer a treat, start placing your hand **without** the treat on the tug.
9. Cue *mine*. As your dog releases the tug, take the tug and then feed your dog a treat.

PART B

1. Begin to move your hand a few inches away from your dog. When you say mine, encourage your dog to move forward a step such that you can take the tug as your dog releases it.
2. Slowly increase the distance your dog moves toward you to deliver the tug to your hand. Use lots of excited praise as your dog catches on to what you want them to do!

PART C

1. Switch from using a treat as the reinforcer to tugging with your dog. At this point, you will ask your dog to release the tug and as soon as they allow you to take it, you will cue them to *get it* again. (The reinforcer for releasing the tug is the cue to grab it again.)
2. Repeat until your dog is confidently taking and releasing the tug on cue.

PART D

1. Move to a larger area and increase the distance your dog brings the tug.
2. Start throwing the tug and have your dog bring it to you.
3. Have your dog wait at your side in a sit or down until you release them to get the tug and bring it back to you.

Puppy Sir working on tugging skills.

Lifelines

- **Dog runs off with the tug** – If your dog tries to keep the tug away from you, attach a light string to it. Hold the string and encourage your dog to calm down and bring the tug to you.
- **Dog runs off with the tug** – If your dog tries to keep the tug away from you, attach a light leash to their flat collar or harness. Hold the leash to keep your dog near you. Don't allow your dog to run off and have an exciting game of keeping the tug away from you.
- **Dog won't trade the tug for a treat** – Try trading an identical or higher value tug that you have kept hidden behind or under you.

Keep your sessions of play short and fun. Celebrate your dog's successes and laugh at their missteps. You will make errors during the games, so cut your dog some slack.

Mission accomplished

You and your dog have now mastered the two foundational enrichment games, Distraction action and the Engagement game. Learning to play the following games is much easier. Really! You and your dog are now playing together like a well-oiled machine, heavy on the fun and light on the oil.

In the Cone squares game, your dog will get to stretch their legs and their mind. It's time to dig out a short see-through barrier and some cones. Contrary to popular belief, squares actually can be quite cool.

Cheat sheet 5#

Cone squares

1. Set up your 8-cone square, barrier, and targets. Use of a home base is optional.
2. Point to move your dog to the target and treat.
3. Reset. Send your dog to the other target.
4. Move targets to the corners of the square.
5. Move targets to the sides of the square.
6. Remove or fade the foot targets.
7. Remove or fade home base.
8. With your hand, guide your dog around the square until you have complete circles.
9. Get your dog circling at a trot.

To win: Dog walks a half circle in both directions with no foot targets.

Level up: Dog trots a full circle in both directions with no home base.

Challenge: _____

CHAPTER 8

Squares can be cool

It's time to get your high-energy dog into action. Not mindless action but thoughtful, intentional activity. The Cone square game is just what your dog has been waiting for and you are not going to be disappointed either.

In Cone squares, you will be introducing your dog to circling around a square of cones. You may be able to play this game inside, since an area about 12 × 12 feet should be sufficient. Make sure to have plenty of clearance around the square so that your dog doesn't run into any furniture or other obstructions.

You will start by using foot targets, so have yours handy – only two foot targets are needed. If you haven't played with foot targets in a while, bring them out and practice sending your dog from one target to the other and then back again, as a refresher.

Go to a mat

Using a mat as a home station will make things clear to your dog as this game progresses. To teach *go to a mat*, you need a mat that your dog can comfortably stand all four feet on. A mat that is a different texture from the surface you are playing on will help your dog know when they are on the mat.

You may also use a slightly raised platform that doesn't slide around. Keep the height of the platform to an inch or two. This will allow your dog to tell when they have all four feet on the platform and when they do not.

Sir standing on a platform.

Don't fence me in

Actually, fencing yourself in is exactly what I have in mind. The point of this game is to get your dog moving around a square of eight cones while you stand in the center of the square. Use whatever you have handy as cones: bowls or buckets turned upside down work well. The only requirement is that the cones are safe for your dog to run into, as that may happen.

To initially keep your dog on the perimeter of the cone square you will also need a barrier of some type. I like to use an X-pen, but any see-through barrier will work. You won't be using the barrier for long, so improvise rather than buy.

The purpose of the barrier is to encourage your dog to stay on the outside of the cone square, so you will be presenting your treat or toy on the outside of the square. The cone square should be approximately 4 × 4 feet in size.

ABOVE: Renn, in South Africa, contemplating Sally Adam's barrier. ABOVE RIGHT: Qwest contemplating Barb's barrier in the US of A!

Moving right along

Now all you need are 20 treats and a treat pouch to hold them. At this point, it is time to switch to using a treat pouch as you will need your hands free to signal your dog.

NOTE: *Decision time! I decided to pull my dog forward by using my right hand as the cue for moving clockwise. All of the images and directions in this book are based on the use of your right hand for clockwise movement. Feel free to use your left hand, if that feels more comfortable for you and your dog. Just remember to consistently either pull or push your dog forward as you play the games.*

Cone square game – right on target

PART A

1. Place two foot targets about 10 feet apart. Stand about 3 feet off of the line between the targets. Your dog will stand directly between the targets and face you.
2. Point to a target with the hand closest to the target. (Frisbees make great targets!)
3. If your dog goes to the target and stands on it, mark and feed a treat. (You may have to lean over to feed the treat while your dog is standing on the target.)
4. If your dog doesn't go to the target, lure them to stand on the target with a treat and then feed the treat.
5. Leave your dog standing on the target and return to your original position.

6. Point to the other target with the hand closest to that target. (The hand you use should be the opposite hand that you used for the first target indication.)
7. If your dog goes to the target and stands on it, mark and feed a treat.
8. If your dog doesn't go to the target, lure them to stand on the target and then feed a treat.
9. Again, leave your dog standing on the target and return to your original position.

10. Start sending your dog from target to target by indicating the next target with your hand point.
11. Send your dog from target to target until all 20 treats have been fed.

HINT: *When indicating a target on your right, use your right hand. As you modify your dog's path from a line to an arc around you, you will continue to use your right hand and turn in a small circle while walking forward.*

PART B

1. Now place your mat or platform (home base) directly between the two targets and have your dog stand on home base. You may need to lure your dog to stand on the mat. Feed several treats while your dog stands on the mat. (Use of a home base is optional.)
2. Return to your original position off to the side of the set up.
3. Point to one target, mark, and treat when your dog stands on that target.

4. Now point to home base, mark, and treat when your dog stands on home base.

5. Send your dog to the other target by pointing to it. Mark and treat when your dog stands on the target.

6. Again, send your dog to home base, mark, and treat.

7. Now send your dog randomly to either target by pointing at it. (**From this point on** you will be marking, probably with a word, and then feeding a treat every time you ask your dog to move to a target or back home.)

8. When your treats are gone, the game is over. Easy peasy!

Unless your dog struggles, play the first two rounds of this game only once or twice and move on to the next level of the game. Feel free to play this game until you and your dog are both comfortable as you send your dog from home base to a target and back to home base again.

Sir on home base.

Initially, I lured Sir by moving my hand to the side and then dropping a treat on the floor.

In this scenario, I am using my foot targets but not a home base.

Because Sir already knew his verbal directionals, I did not need to use my hands to point at the targets. You will need to point to indicate which target your dog is to go to.

Cone square game – a moving target

PART A

1. Grab 20 more treats and set up your 8 cones in a square, approximately 4 × 4 feet in size. Place your barrier along the front or completely around the cone square. Add your home base directly in the center of the front of the cone square and your targets a few feet out to the side. (See pictures on pages 78 and 79 for setup.)
2. You stand in the center of the cone square and your dog stands on home base facing you.
3. Point to a target, mark and treat with your dog standing on the target.
4. Point to home base and have your dog move back home.

5. Point to the other target and have your dog move to that target.

6. Now send your dog back to home base with a hand point.
7. When your dog is comfortable going to either target and then back to home base, it is time to move the targets to a new position.

PART B

1. Place your targets just around the corner of the cone square. Make sure your dog can still see the targets from home base. (See picture below right.)
2. Follow the steps from Part A, above and send your dog from home base to each target randomly and then back to home base.
3. When your dog is comfortable, move the targets to the middle of the sides of the cone square. (Your dog may no longer be able to see the targets from home base.)

4. From now on, instead of just pointing at a target, you want to lead your dog to the target by swinging your arm from near your dog to over the target. (Basically, you will be sweeping your arm from your dog to the target.)
5. Once you have fed a treat, sweep your other arm back to home base and have your dog station themselves on home base again.

6. Randomly send your dog to either foot target and then back to home base.
7. Play this version of the game until you and your dog are confidently playing.

Now it is time to fade your foot targets. You may keep using a home base for a while but your foot targets are history.

Setup with targets moving around the side of the cone square with Sir in home position. *Now Sir is moving around the barrier to get to the targets on each side.*

Cone square game – a disappearing target

PART A

1. This game is just like the previous one, except you are going to remove your foot targets. Grab another 20 treats.
2. The setup is the same as the previous game, but you are no longer using any foot targets.
3. Stand in the center of your cone square and get your dog settled on home base.
4. Sweep your right arm to the right, as if the foot target was still present on the right side of the cone square.
5. When your dog starts following your hand signal, mark and treat. Your dog only has to take a step or two to earn their treat.
6. Send your dog back to home base with your left hand.

7. Again, send your dog to the right with your sweeping hand signal and have your dog go all the way around to the middle of the right side of the cone square. (If your dog doesn't go as far as you indicated, offer your treat over the spot that you indicated.)
8. Now send your dog back to home base. Start sending your dog to the middle of the left side of the cone square using your left hand.

PART B

1. Once your dog is going to the middle of each side of the cone square and back home again, you can send your dog even farther.
2. Follow the same steps as in Part A of this level of the game, but send your dog farther and farther around the cone square by sweeping your arm ahead of your dog. (Turn your body and lead your dog around with your hand.)
3. Have your dog go around on both sides until they are going all the way to the back of the cone square. Your dog will return to home base after each repetition.
4. Then send your dog to the same side or the opposite side.

PART C

1. Now you will start taking your dog farther and farther along each side until you are finally taking them from home base, around the cone square, and back to home base. (Ping pong how far you ask your dog to go each time. Sometimes have your dog go one third of the way around, then two thirds, then one third, and then all of the way.)
2. Eventually, lead your dog randomly, either clockwise or counter-clockwise, around the square.

PART D

1. Remove home base.
2. Position your dog where home base used to be and have them go around the square in each direction. Repeat until your dog is comfortable not using a home base in the setup.
3. Now, start your dog at random places around the cone square and have them circle up to one complete revolution around the square.
4. Have your dog go randomly in both directions, following the sweep of your hand.
5. Now sweep your arm a bit faster and get your dog trotting around the cone square, in both directions. Give your dog some verbal encouragement if they are reluctant to move from a walk to a trot.

6. The final step is to remove your see-through barrier. Since you have fed all of your treats outside of the cone square, your dog should not be pushing to come into the center of the square with you.

HINT: *To get your dog moving faster, instead of delivering the treat to your dog's mouth, toss it on the floor just ahead of your dog.*

You and your dog are now playing this game with only cones and treats. You have removed both of the foot targets and the home base. Eventually, you will go back to using foot targets in more advanced games but you can put them away for now.

HINT: *When sending your dog back in the opposite direction, switch hands. Always use the same hand for clockwise circling and your other hand for counter-clockwise circling.*

As you transition from short arcs to sending your dog in full circles, your arm position changes. When you send your dog almost straight from one target to another, your arm is straight out and in line with your shoulders. Once your dog starts to curve around you, turn your body toward your sweeping arm so that your arm is at a 90° angle to your body. Ninety degrees is not a magic number! Find the angle that is comfortable and works best for you and your dog. For safety, turn so you are walking forward rather than backward. You want to see where both you and your dog are going.

The great thing about the games is that you are
not only developing a dog who pays laser attention
to you but a dog with tremendous self-control.

Well done!

Cheat sheet #6

Cone circles

1. Transition your cone square to a cone circle.
2. Enlarge the cone circle and get your dog trotting or cantering around it.
3. Go back to having your dog walk the circle.
4. Add sits, downs, and other behaviors.
5. Add obstacles, one type at a time, such as low jumps or foot targets.
6. Increase your dog's speed from a walk to a trot or a gallop.

To win: Dog moves around large cone circle in both directions at speed and negotiates one type of obstacle such as jumps.

Level up: Dog circles in both directions, following verbal cues.

Challenge: _____

_____

CHAPTER 9

Running in circles can move your dog ahead

Does your dog always seem to have an unlimited supply of energy and enthusiasm? Burning off some of that extra energy, while keeping your dog in thinking mode, is the objective of the Cone circle game. You simply give verbal or physical cues while your dog moves in response to those cues. Put another way, you stand and orchestrate and your dog plays around you.

Your dog will be moving at speed while playing this game, so it is strongly suggested that you warm up your dog before starting. You will also want to have a cool-down routine in place for when you are done playing games.

HINT: *Contact your veterinarian to help you set up appropriate warm-up and cool-down routines that are tailored to your dog.*

Square-to-circle transition

You will need a large area, preferably outdoors, to move from the Cone square game to the Cone circle game. Start out by moving your small cone square from inside to outside in a fenced area, if possible. Play the Cone

Renn exercising.

square game from the beginning to the final stage. This will refresh your dog's memory and get them used to playing the game in a new environment.

Once your dog is confidently playing the Cone square game outside, start enlarging the square a little at a time. Stay aware of any obstacles in your play area such as trees, lawn furniture, or uneven ground that may pose a hazard to your dog.

HINT: *Your dog will soon be running, so plan for them to swing out beyond your cone square or circle.*

There are two ways to transition from cone squares to cone circles. You can either change your small cone square to a circle and *then* expand it, or you can expand your cone square and *then* change it to a circle. The change from a square to a circular shape is so minor that your dog should adapt to this change without any problem.

HINT: *Cones delineate the playing area, but your dog is more interested in playing the games than the shape of the cone setup.*

Paula Stone and Arya of the UK using a large flirt pole to play the Cone circle game.

Enlarge the circle

Let's start with a small cone square. Have your dog play the Cone square game until they are comfortable playing outside. Now move four of the eight cones outward to form a small cone circle. Play a few rounds of the Cone square game using your new cone circle setup.

Slowly enlarge the circle until it nearly fills your play area. Stand inside the cone circle and set your dog up facing you, both of you will be standing. Stretch a hand out toward your dog and turn toward your hand such that you can walk forward in a small circle. Your dog should then follow your outstretched hand around the circle. Be sure to circle your dog in both directions.

SUPER HINT: Remember, when using your hand as a physical cue for circling, think of either pulling or pushing your dog with your hand. Once you decide on pushing or pulling, stick with that hand signal!

Remember for pulling to use your right hand for clockwise circles and your left hand for counterclockwise circles. Also, always walk forward as you move with your dog. For pushing, use your left hand for clockwise and your right for counter-clockwise.

HINT: *At this point, it is easiest to use a tug or ball as a reinforcer. Large treats that you can toss can also be used. A flirt pole is best saved for later use.*

Cone circle game – *intro level*

PART A

1. Set up your cone circle, paying close attention to obstructions that are present in your play area. (A fenced yard is ideal.)
2. Grab a toy or treats that you can throw with precision. (Keep your toy or treat hidden until you are ready to throw it.)
3. You will stand in the middle with your dog on the perimeter of the circle.
4. Have your dog stop in any position; sit, stand, or down.
5. Raise your hand toward your dog and turn your body perpendicular to your dog as you both prepare to circle.

6. Release your dog with a cue such as *let's go*, if necessary. If your dog will start moving without a verbal cue, that is fine too.
7. Sweep your arm to keep your dog circling as you turn your body and walk forward in a small circle. Circle up to one full circle.
8. When you want your dog to stop, stop your movement and drop your hand to your side.

9. When your dog stops on the perimeter, mark and throw your treat or toy outside of the cone circle. (Your dog may enter the cone circle to bring the toy to you.)

10. Reset your dog back on the circle perimeter either by sending them back out or by walking with them.

11. Send your dog in the opposite direction around the circle and repeat the above steps. (Your dog has now gone both directions around the circle.)

12. Repeat the above steps until your dog is confidently circling.

PART B

1. Repeat Part A and encourage your dog to increase their speed one gait as they circle by jogging in a small circle and using a happy voice to encourage them to increase their pace from a walk to a trot or from a trot to a canter.

2. After marking for increased speed, throw your toy or treat to the outside of the circle and *ahead* of your dog so that your dog chases the toy or treat.

3. Soon your dog will be cueing primarily off of the speed of your hand sweep in determining how fast they move around the circle. Take a break!

PART C

1. So far your dog hasn't had to do much thinking when playing the Cone circle game, but that is about to change. Now you will be adding sit and down to the game.

2. Continue to play this game as outlined above, but now when you stop your dog you will ask for a *sit* or a *down* before you mark and throw your toy.

PART D

1. Once your dog gets into the flow of this game you can really get your dog thinking by asking for two stationary behaviors before reinforcing.

2. Next you can ask for a stationary behavior, such as *sit*, *down*, or *stand*, and then send your dog on a full or partial circle.

3. Now ask for your dog to circle, stop, *sit*, *down*, *sit*, and circle again in the same direction or the opposite direction. (See the lifelines below on tips to get your dog to stop circling.) The possibilities are endless!

HINT: *To get your dog stopping, stop your movement and drop your hand to your side. Since your dog is following your hand and body, stopping your movement cues them to stop.*

HINT: *Ask for a full or partial circle, a half or three-quarters of a circle, at speed, but don't have your dog go round and round circling. If your dog gets orbiting, they tend to quit thinking and start running mindlessly.*

Lifelines

- **Dog comes into the center of the circle** – If your dog doesn't stay on the perimeter of the circle, collapse your circle back to a very small size and put up barriers to encourage your dog to stay on the perimeter. Fade the barriers by lowering, shrinking, or removing alternate barriers until they are completely gone. (Barriers that you might use include an X-pen or PVC pipe from cone to cone.)
- **Dog continues to move around the circle instead of stopping** – Encourage your dog to slow down to a walk or trot around the circle by slowing your movements and using a calm, soft voice. If your dog is moving slower, they are more likely to stop when asked. Once your dog is stopping when asked, start increasing the speed they travel around the circle.
- **Dog continues to move around the circle instead of stopping** – If your dog doesn't stop when you stop and drop your hand, turn and face your dog and then turn in the opposite direction. As soon as your dog stops to turn in the other direction, mark and hand your dog a reinforcer. Once your dog is stopping when asked, fade your change in body position until you are just dropping your hand to indicate a stop.

You can ramp up the thinking aspect of this game by adding any tricks or behaviors that your dog knows such as bow, back, wave, or beg to the game.

To play the next level of the Circle game, you will need to gather a few more pieces of equipment. Let your imagination guide you as you select gear.

Gold changing circling directions without stopping.

On cue

This is a good place to add verbal cues for circling clockwise and counterclockwise.

HINT: *Always think of circling as your dog moving either clockwise or counterclockwise as you would see it if you were looking down from above, such as the view from a plane or drone.*

Once your dog is following your hand sweep, it is fairly easy to add a verbal cue to these behaviors. First you need to decide on the cues you will use. I suggest *circle* for clockwise and *arc* for anti-clockwise or counterclockwise. The C of *circle* matches the C of clockwise and the A of *arc* matches the A of anti-clockwise.

Once you decide on cues, the procedure is to place the new verbal cue just before the old physical cue of your hand sweep or new cue > old cue. Make sure to pause slightly between delivering your new verbal cue and the arm sweep, the old physical cue.

On cue – adding a verbal cue

PART A

1. Decide which verbal cues you want to use for each circling direction. (I suggest *circle* for clockwise and *arc* for anti- or counterclockwise. Think of the directions as if you are looking down from above.)
2. Set up a small 8 cone circle and grab 20 treats.
3. Circle your dog all the way around in each direction.
4. Pick one direction to start adding a cue to that direction.

5. Let's start with *circle* or clockwise. (You may also start with *arc*.)
6. Have your dog circle a quarter circle clockwise by following your arm sweep. Mark and treat.
7. Repeat 3 more times, circling a quarter circle clockwise. (Your dog will now be back where they started.)
8. Now say *circle*, pause a moment, and then add the arm sweep. Take your dog a quarter circle, mark, and treat.
9. Repeat 3 more times, always taking your dog clockwise. (Be sure to include the short pause between the verbal cue and the hand sweep.)

10. Now pause a beat or two longer between your circle cue and your hand sweep.
11. If your dog turns their head or steps in the correct clockwise direction, immediately mark and treat. Yay!
12. If your dog just stands and looks at you, repeat steps 5 through 11.
13. Once your dog is looking or stepping in the correct direction when cued, wait for them to go a bit farther. (If they only turned their head, wait for a step and if they took a step, wait for another step.)
14. When your dog starts circling on your verbal cue, drop your physical arm sweep.

15. Soon your dog will be moving off confidently on only the verbal cue circle. You have now added a verbal cue to one circling direction!
16. Do a few more sessions concentrating on the clockwise cue. (Take breaks between sessions.)

PART B

1. Go back and add the other circling cue by following steps 5 through 16 using the cue *arc* and having your dog circle counterclockwise.
2. Once your dog is confidently going in both directions, start mixing up the cues.
3. If your dog struggles, go back and work on one cue by itself and then add the other cue back in.
4. When your dog takes both cues confidently, when given in random order, you have achieved lift-off!

Congrats! You have added verbal cues! Your dog now knows how to circle in either direction without needing physical cues from you. You can switch your physical *stop* cue to a verbal cue by repeating the above exercise and adding the verbal *stop* cue before you physically signal your dog to stop. Practice until your dog will circle in both directions without you moving a muscle, except maybe your lips.

From now on, you can use either verbal cues or physical hand sweeps to cue your dog to circle. Verbal cues come in very handy when you start using a flirt pole. Using a hand sweep while holding a flirt pole is tricky, so do yourself and your dog a favor by putting the circling directions on verbal cues. Now you are ready to move on to a more complicated **Cone circle** game.

First you will need to gather up a bit more game gear. Look around your home and pull together gear that you can add to this game. (See suggestions on the next page.) Try setting up new obstacles away from the cone circle. Your dog should be proficient at negotiating the obstacle(s) before you add them to your cone circle.

Suggested gear for the advanced Cone circle **game**

- Foot targets – Mats, platforms, or Frisbees.
- Cavalettis – Sets of four or six very low jumps set up in sequence which your dog trots over.
- Low jumps – Use your imagination to construct low jumps. A light bar on two overturned bowls, oatmeal boxes, or cones can be used as a jump.
- Platforms – Low with good footing and large enough for your dog to stand on comfortably.

Game setup

Before adding new obstacles to the Cone circle game, ensure that your dog is comfortable interacting with them away from the cone circle. Then position the new obstacles at the distance your dog typically circles the cones. Allow your dog to learn to confidently interact with each obstacle type before adding other types.

By introducing new obstacles in this way, your dog will encounter them naturally while circling the cones, rather than having to veer off course to navigate them. With patience and practice, your dog will become skilled at negotiating all obstacles in the Cone circle game.

Add new obstacles one at a time so your dog learns how to interact with each type of obstacle before adding a new type. For example, if you start by adding a foot target, play the game with only foot targets; if you first add target mats, only once your dog is comfortable with going to and standing on the mats, should you add a new type of obstacle such as cavalettis or low jumps.

Sir negotiating low jumps.

HINT: *Start by adding obstacles that your dog is used to interacting with. Later add unfamiliar obstacles away from and then to your cone setup. All obstacles should be familiar to your dog before being added to your cone circle setup.*

When you introduce jumps or platforms to the game, start with the jump bars on the ground or use very low platforms. When your dog is easily negotiating the obstacle as they are circling at speed, you can increase its height, if desired.

Cone circle game – *advanced level*

PART A

1. Use the cone circle setup from the **Intro level** game plan above.
2. Add new, but familiar, types of obstacles one at a time. Only add obstacles that your dog can safely negotiate and are age and ability appropriate for your dog. (You can add several obstacles at once, but have all of them be the same type of obstacle, like all foot targets or low jumps.)
3. Set the new obstacle(s) quite close to the cone circle if your dog will hold their speed to a walk around the cone circle. If your dog tends to trot or run, place your new obstacle(s) a bit farther from the cone circle.

4. Play the game slowly and allow your dog to carefully interact with the new obstacle(s).
5. Once your dog is confidently negotiating the obstacle(s), you may add a new type of obstacle.

6. Continue adding obstacles until your setup is complete.
7. Encourage your dog to move slowly around the circle as they engage with each obstacle to grow their confidence.

PART B

1. Once your dog is safely circling your setup at a slow, comfortable pace, it is time to consider changing your setup slightly.
2. As your dog moves faster, they may travel farther out from the cone circle. You may need to move your obstacles a few feet farther away from the circle, so make that adjustment, if necessary.

3. Now ask your dog to speed up a bit and see how they interact with the obstacles around the circle.

4. Adjust the spacing between obstacles and the distance of each obstacle from the cone circle. You want to make it easy for your dog to move around the circle and negotiate each obstacle.

1. Write down or mentally note which obstacles work well, which are not so great for your dog, and what distance from the circle and from other obstacles, works best for each type of obstacle.

2. **Play on!** Now that you have optimized your game setup, you are ready for lots of fun with your dog. You can guide your dog around the circle and over obstacles while indicating when you want them to stop and telling them what you would like them to do while they are stopped.

3. Keep the game fresh by changing up what you ask your dog to do and when you ask them to do it. This will keep your dog listening as they will never be sure exactly when you will ask them to circle, stop, negotiate an obstacle, or perform a stationary behavior.

If you find any of the obstacles unsafe or problematic, remove them. Set up the games solely for your and your dog's enjoyment. Eventually, you can add other obstacles such as cavalettis or tunnels as transitions from one circle to another, but not quite yet!

Advanced cone circle with multiple circles and obstacles.

Problem obstacles include:
- Your dog isn't comfortable negotiating the obstacle.
- The obstacle isn't stable or safe.
- The obstacle just isn't much fun for your dog.

That covers the **Cone circle** game and brings us to the end of the **Green grass** games. As promised, the next chapter will introduce the **Blue sky** games and the joys of using a flirt pole in your games. A flirt pole is my absolute favorite piece of gear for gameplay. I hope you will give flirt pole play a test drive and allow your dog to show you that playing with a flirt pole is squirrel-chasing level fun.

LEVEL 2 BLUE SKY GAMES

Cheat sheet #7

Flirt pole fun

1. Practice flirt pole basics without your dog.
2. Get your dog grabbing and then releasing the squirrel.
3. Introduce the stop cue when using the flirt pole.
4. Teach the difference between a release cue and a marker cue. (*Get it* vs *yes*.)
5. Add your verbal stop cue.
6. Keep your dog moving freely to grab the squirrel but ready to stop when cued.

To win: Dog grabs the squirrel when released to get it.

Level up: Dog stops and then grabs the squirrel when cued.

Challenge: _____

_____

_____

CHAPTER 10

The game your dog won't want to miss

Has your dog ever chased a squirrel? Or wanted to? How about a cat, a bird, or a car? Most dogs are pre-programmed to hunt and catch prey. That means they are going to chase it. Chasing prey is hard-wired in your dog and can cause a lot of headaches for you. How would you like to harness this strong instinctual drive and make it your best friend instead of your worst nightmare?

Welcome to the **Flirt pole** game! First, you will learn the basics of playing with a flirt pole – the stop and go. I like to use the cue *walk* because you will usually want your dog to be walking for this part of the game. Of course, the flirt pole will later be introduced in the **Go fish** game, where you will have your dog moving at speed. For now, let's look at how to safely play with a flirt pole and the basic skills of stop and go.

Using a flirt pole allows you to control "prey" and limit your dog's access to it. You decide when your dog is allowed to chase and grab the toy squirrel. The best part about using a flirt pole is that your dog really sees the toy on the end of it as prey.

Sir playing with a flirt pole. Note that the toy is attached to a string that is connected to a long handle.

Most of the games in this book can be played using a flirt pole. If you already use a flirt pole, you will find that enrichment games will take your flirt pole play to a whole new, stratospheric level. Flirt poles are my favorite toy because they are my dogs' favorite toy. Flirt pole play should be super fun for you and your dog.

Safety first

A flirt pole can be a lot of fun for your dog as long as you keep your dog safe while playing with it. To play safely, you need to keep the squirrel either on the ground or out of your dog's reach. You do not want your dog jumping and twisting to grab the squirrel or they could hurt themselves.

HINT: *Always remember that your dog thinks they are chasing prey, the flirt pole toy, and they will do almost anything to catch that darn escaping prey.*

When playing with a flirt pole you have to know what actions to take and to take them immediately. Practicing without your dog is crucial. You can't be standing there thinking about what to do next because, believe me, your dog isn't going to wait for you to make a thoughtful decision. They will be charging to get the toy or squirrel, if it's within reach.

If you ever get flustered while playing with your dog and a flirt pole, your default choice should be to fly the squirrel back into your hand where it is not accessible to your dog. One hand holds the handle of the flirt pole rod and the other should be free to grab the squirrel when you fly it back to you. A flying squirrel!

Basic flirt pole play

The Flirt pole game is based on permission. Your dog has permission to chase and grab the squirrel or they do not. Let's look at a simple example: You have the squirrel stationary on the ground and have asked your dog to sit. Your dog sits nicely so you release them to grab the squirrel while pulling the toy away from them. They grab the toy and you have a tug session with them.

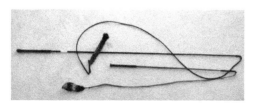

Two sizes of flirt poles. One is a Tail Teaser and the other made from a horse lunge whip with a toy attached. For a link to purchase a Tail Teaser flirt pole see the Resources section at the back of this book.

The alternate scenario is that after you ask your dog to sit, they try to grab the squirrel instead of sitting. If they grab the squirrel before you remove it, they have learned that your cues are not that important. They can get what they want even if they ignore you. But, if you are ready and fly the squirrel high up over your dog's head and back into your free hand, you have prevented your dog from grabbing the squirrel without permission.

Your dog will begin to understand that you control their access to the squirrel and if they want it, they need to listen to you. The key is to make quick decisions and take immediate action to allow your dog to either grab the toy or prevent them from snatching it.

To buy or not to buy

The flirt pole is the only piece of equipment that I suggest you buy. You can make a flirt pole out of a wooden handle and assorted other items you might have around your home, but it is difficult to replicate the spring in the flexible rod of a purchased pole.

HINT: *Do yourself and your dog a favor and purchase a flirt pole with a flexible handle. They are not very expensive and make playing with them much more fun, while being easier on your shoulders and arms.*

Before you purchase a flirt pole, try putting a toy on a string, with or without the string being attached to a pole, and get your dog to play with it. If your dog will chase a toy pulled along the ground on a string, they will engage with a flirt pole.

What I particularly like about flirt poles is that they provide a spring-like tension when your dog is tugging on the toy, which makes the toy come to life! This ability to flex also makes it easier on your dog's mouth and your hands and arms. Another win-win!

Before you start

No matter what flirt pole you use, you need to be proficient in handling it. You want to be able to place the toy where you want it to go, move it along the ground such that it either runs or dances, and then fly it back into your free hand with ease.

Target practice is a fun, easy way to gain the skills needed to handle a flirt pole. Since this practice is used to hone your skills in handling the flirt pole, your dog shouldn't be present while you are refining your flirt pole skills.

Flirt pole target practice.

For targets, you can use anything from bowls to Frisbees or hula hoops. The precision flirt pole skills that you need to practice include:

- Have the toy hit a target, while holding the flirt pole in either hand.
- Fly the toy back to your free hand, and practice catching using both hands.
- Pull the toy along the ground and make it run or dance.
- Practice all flirt pole skills with small and large flirt poles, if you have both.
- Practice walking around as you manipulate the flirt pole

You will quickly gain proficiency with a small flirt pole, but a large flirt pole requires a bit more practice to use precisely.

Sir is just about to grab the toy or squirrel.

Flirt pole game – the grab

1. Set a timer for 5 minutes.
2. Flip the squirrel onto the ground.
3. Immediately give your release cue (*get it*).
4. If your dog does not go over and grab the squirrel, use the flirt pole handle to move it along the ground and away from your dog, which makes it seem to come alive. Get excited and verbally encourage your dog to grab it!

---

5. Once your dog grabs the squirrel let them tug for a moment while you hold the handle.
6. Ask your dog to release the squirrel just as you would a tug.
7. Repeat this 5 times.
8. Take a break!

This should be a no-brainer for your dog. If your dog has ever chased anything in their life, they should be enthusiastic about chasing the squirrel.

Lifelines

- **Dog is reluctant to grab the squirrel** – Always pull the toy away from your dog, prey (almost) never runs toward your dog.
- **Dog is reluctant to grab the squirrel** – Try using a toy attached to a string, as your dog may find the pole intimidating. Once your dog is readily grabbing the squirrel, add the toy to a flirt pole.
- **Dog won't release the squirrel** – Practice the release of a toy away from the Flirt pole game. Trade a toy for an identical toy or a great treat to encourage the release of the toy.
- **Dog won't release the squirrel** – Try giving the toy your dog is holding a gentle push toward your dog before you ask them to release it. Most dogs don't want the prey to push against them. The game is only fun if the prey is trying to escape.

HINT: *If your dog struggles to get enthused about playing with a flirt pole toy, try changing the toy to their favorite toy, even a ball on a rope or a Frisbee with a small hole to attach a string will work. An empty plastic water bottle may be a super attractive squirrel for dogs that love to crunch!*

Now is a good time to add a verbal *stop* to your dog's cues, if you haven't yet done so.

Flirt pole game – the stop

PART A

1. Stand facing your dog while holding your flirt pole, one hand holding the handle and the other hand holding the squirrel.
2. Flip the squirrel onto the ground about 6 feet in front of your dog.
3. As your dog moves towards the squirrel (and they may move very quickly, so be ready), flip the squirrel off of the ground and back over your dog's head and onto the ground behind them before they can grab the squirrel. You don't want to say anything to your dog. Just flip the squirrel high above your dog's head so that they do not attempt to leap up and grab the squirrel as it passes over them. (Your dog should immediately turn around and attempt to grab the squirrel again.)

4. Keep flying the squirrel over your dog's head and landing it behind them until they stop trying to get it and stand still.
5. The moment your dog stops, release them to the squirrel with *get it*. Then tug with your dog and reset them for the next repetition.
6. Repeat this several more times and grow the time your dog waits for the release until your dog is waiting 5 seconds for you to release them to get the squirrel.

PART B

1. When your dog stops on the next trial, mark the stop with *yes*, but do **not** say *get it* this time.
2. If your dog holds the stop, give your release cue *get it* and allow them to grab the squirrel, tug, and reset.
3. If your dog releases on *yes*, whip the squirrel high over their head and repeat step 2 until your dog holds their stop when marked. Then release your dog to the squirrel with *get it*.
4. When your dog is consistently waiting for the release cue after the mark, celebrate and take a long break!

 HINT: *The squirrel does **not** have to touch the ground in order to be flipped away from your dog. In fact, you want to re-loft the squirrel as soon as you see your dog starting toward it, if they don't have permission to grab it.*

If you have a *stop* on verbal cue, you may find that your dog "forgets" it once the squirrel appears – just follow the directions below to refresh and strengthen that cue.

Lifelines

- **Dog gives up** – If your dog gives up trying to get the squirrel, go back to playing with the flirt pole toy as you would a tug and build more value for the squirrel.
- **Dog gives up** – Sometimes a dog will get discouraged if you are not consistent with your use of your marker and release words. If this happens, go back to practicing without your dog until you get your mechanics perfected.
- **Dog leaps into the air** – Use a long flirt pole and practice flipping the squirrel high into the air. The squirrel does not have to land very far behind your dog, so work on the height, rather than the length, of the squirrel's flight.
- **Dog gets the squirrel before released** – If your dog beats you a time or two, they will work a lot harder to get the squirrel. Be ready to re-loft the squirrel the moment it comes down as most dogs will not wait for the squirrel to land before going after it.

Flirt pole game – the cue

PART A

1. Once you have a solid stop, start to say your cue, *stop*, as you flip the squirrel onto the ground.
2. If your dog stops, mark with *yes* and then release with *get it*.
3. If your dog takes the word *stop* as a release cue, loft the squirrel and land it behind them.
4. Repeat until your dog is not going after the squirrel when cued to stop.

PART B

1. Now flip the squirrel as far in front of your dog as possible, saying *stop* as you do. You want to extend the distance between your dog and the squirrel in front of them. Your dog should stop and wait. If not, re-loft the squirrel until they stop and wait when you say *stop*.
2. When your dog stops when cued, mark with *yes* and tell your dog to *get it*.

3. Next, release your dog and stop them as soon as they start toward the squirrel. The sooner you catch your dog in motion the better.
4. If your dog stops, mark with *yes* and immediately tell them to *get it*, tug, and reset.
5. If your dog ignores the *stop* cue, loft the squirrel and start again.
6. Repeat until your dog will stop and hold the stop on their way to get the squirrel *after* being released to get the squirrel.

PART C

1. An alternative to releasing your dog to grab the squirrel is for you to flip the squirrel back to your dog while they are stopped and give your release word just as the squirrel flies back to them. Then tug and reset.
2. Randomly release your dog to grab the squirrel and to fly it back to them. Remember to always use your release cue *get it* in both situations. Always tug and reset after your dog earns the squirrel!
3. Take a break and celebrate!

Play this game with your dog until your dog will stop when they are about to grab the squirrel. Then play it until your dog will run right up to the squirrel and wait only inches from it for their release cue before they grab the squirrel. If you are consistent, you will be amazed how quickly your dog will get to this point!

Lifelines

- **Dog gives up trying to get the squirrel** – If your dog pauses when released or quits trying to get the squirrel, go back to the Flirt pole game – the grab until they get back into the game. Until your dog learns that they will eventually get the squirrel, they may become frustrated and not want to play. Don't wait until your dog quits playing to go back to the grab!
- **Dog won't wait for the release cue when close to the squirrel** – If your dog usually does well waiting for the release cue but not when they are close, you need to be really quick to flip the squirrel out of their grasp so they cannot self-reinforce by grabbing it when no release cue is given. Ping pong the distance you ask your dog to stop as they approach the toy.

Walk on

Now that your dog is able to stop around a dancing squirrel, you want to get them moving. What fun is it to have a flying squirrel if your dog only gets to stop and look at it? Don't wait too long to move on from the stop to get your dog moving as you don't want your dog to associate the squirrel only with stopping and chasing. The squirrel has a lot more tricks up their sleeve that your dog will want to learn.

 HINT: *Quickly move on from teaching the* stop *to getting your dog walking toward the toy or your dog may become reluctant to walk or stalk the squirrel.*

You will be doing things a bit differently when teaching your dog to walk toward the squirrel. Instead of adding the cue later, you will be adding a prompt early and later changing the prompt to a cue.
Don't worry, you will learn exactly what to say and when to say it to keep it clear in your mind and easy for your dog to learn.

Let's keep moving along!

Cheat sheet #8

Squirrel on the loose

1. Flip the squirrel out in front of your dog and release your dog to the squirrel.
2. As soon as your dog takes a step, mark and release your dog to get the squirrel and reset.
3. Grow the number of steps your dog walks.
4. Add the distance your dog stalks toward the squirrel as you also walk forward.
5. Change verbal cue from *let's go* to *walk*.
6. Add your flirt pole to the Cone Circle Game.
7. Drop squirrel down to the ground.

To win: Dog walks toward the squirrel, stops, and grabs it on cue.

Level up: Flirt pole or tug used in place of treats in enrichment games.

Challenge: _____

_____

CHAPTER 11

A fast and furious game

You and your dog are halfway to squirrelly success. Your dog now knows how to stop and then grab a squirrel so it is time to get them stalking that darn varmint. Stalking prey comes natural to most dogs so you will have nature on your side for this part of the game.

HINT: *Focus on having fun! Take a break if you or your dog starts to get frustrated. Learning a game can be challenging.*

If you find your dog is reticent to freely move toward the squirrel, go back to releasing and then allowing them to grab the squirrel. Still not very enthused? Then pull the squirrel away from your dog as soon as you release them to grab it.

Sir walking toward the toy.

Flirt pole game – the walk

PART A

1. Stand facing the same direction as your dog while holding the flirt pole.
2. Your dog should be facing the same direction that you are but off to one side and 3 feet behind you.
3. Flip the squirrel out 6 feet in front of your dog.
4. Encourage your dog forward with the prompt *let's go* or another release word.

---

5. When your dog takes a step forward toward the squirrel, mark with *yes* and release them to the squirrel with *get it*.
6. Tug with your dog and reset.
7. Repeat marking one step 3 times. Then withhold your marker word and wait for your dog to take two steps.

PART B

1. Start ping-ponging the number of forward steps you ask for before marking until you get up to 10 steps. You may have to pull the squirrel forward on the ground to make room for your dog to walk 10 steps forward. If your dog tries to grab the squirrel when it starts to move, flip it back into your hand and start again.
2. Start walking forward, dragging the squirrel off to the side and in front of your dog as your dog walks forward.

---

3. Now work the same exercise with you on the other side of your dog.
4. Take a break!

At this point, your dog should be freely walking forward, not pausing or stuttering. When you start to move the squirrel away from your dog, they may freeze, lunge, keep walking, or slow down. All of these are normal reactions to the prey coming alive or moving, so be ready to fly the squirrel back into your free hand if your dog reacts in any manner other than continuing to walk forward.

Always mark while your dog is moving freely. Don't be afraid to withhold a mark if your dog gets sticky or very slow. In the long run, it is easier to slow a dog down than speed them up. As your dog approaches the prey, they will tend to slow down. Your dog is getting more cautious because the closer they get to the prey, the more likely it is that the prey will try to run and escape. They want to sneak up on the squirrel to improve their chances of catching it.

Watch out for your dog getting sticky, which means slowing down significantly, when the squirrel starts moving. Mark moving feet!

Your dog may slow down as they approach the squirrel, but keep marking moving feet.

HINT: *Always remember that your dog really does believe that the toy squirrel is prey because its movement imitates live prey!*

Lifelines

* **Dog gets stuck when squirrel moves** – If your dog freezes or slows down significantly when the squirrel moves, flip the squirrel back into your hand, and pause 10 seconds. Then reset and try again. After a few tries your dog should be able to take a confident step or two forward, so be ready to mark, release, and have a squirrel tug party!
* **Dog lunges at stationary squirrel** – If your dog dives for the squirrel while it is stationary, whip it back into your hand, pause for 10 seconds, and reset. After a few reps your dog should start to walk forward, in which case you can continue with the exercise. If your dog instead gets stuck standing still, encourage them forward by softly prompting *let's go*. Once your dog takes a step or two forward be ready to mark, release, and have a squirrel tug party!

- **Dog lunges when squirrel moves** – If your dog dives for the squirrel when it starts moving, be ready to whip it back into your hand before your dog can grab it. You need to be focused and on your toes, especially while playing with a moving squirrel!
- **Dog is sticky** – Dogs get slower and more cautious as they get closer to prey or as prey moves. If you have trouble with your dog being sticky when walking in, try allowing more distance separating them and the squirrel by *starting* with more distance between your dog and the squirrel.

Now it is time to add to the distance that your dog walks toward the squirrel. At this point, you will need to use a large flirt pole – a large flirt pole is just a horse lunge whip with a toy on the end (purchased from a farm store or on a farm store website).

Flirt pole game – add distance

PART A

1. Stand facing the same direction as your dog while holding the flirt pole.
2. Your dog should be facing the same direction as you are but off to one side and 3 feet behind you.
3. Flip the squirrel out 15 feet in front of your dog. (You will need to use a long flirt pole.)

---

4. Encourage your dog forward with the prompt *let's go*.
5. If your dog starts forward as soon as you say *let's go* and keeps walking steadily toward the squirrel for about 10 feet, or two thirds of the distance to the squirrel, then mark and release to the squirrel. Tug and reset.

PART B

1. If your dog starts forward as soon as you say *let's go* but stops before they get two thirds of the way to the squirrel, flip the squirrel back into your hand, and pause for 10 seconds. Reset your dog to try again.
2. If your dog got stuck partway to the squirrel, note that point and mark, release, and tug a step or two *before* that spot on the next trial.

---

3. Shape your dog to walk all 10 feet by withholding your mark and ping-ponging how many steps or how far you ask your dog to walk without stopping or pausing.
4. Once your dog will walk two thirds of the way to the squirrel without stopping, after starting when prompted, you are ready to start walking along with your dog.

PART C

1. Now walk 10 steps forward while you drag the squirrel on the ground in front of your dog as they walk toward the squirrel. Your 10 steps should increase the distance your dog walks in on the squirrel by 10 steps from step 4 above.
2. You will handle your dog's success or failure exactly as you did previously. The only difference is that now you and the squirrel are moving as your dog walks forward.
3. Be sure to work this with your dog on both sides of you and at different distances from you.

---

4. Start inserting your *walk* cue before *let's go* and when your dog begins to walk forward on the *walk* cue then drop the *let's go* prompt.
5. Take a break!

The key to this exercise is ending the trial if your dog stops walking before you mark and release them to grab the squirrel. It should be easy to change over to the new cue once you have the walk established.

To add your verbal *walk* cue say your new cue (*walk*) before your old cue (*Let's go*), then pause between the two cues to give your dog a chance to respond to the new cue. Once your dog starts walking forward on the new cue, just drop the old cue.

HINT: *The goal is for your dog to start walking when cued and to continue walking toward the squirrel until you cue them to do something else.*

Once your dog can walk forward while you walk 10 steps, start mixing things up to get your dog thinking. Have your dog walk toward the squirrel from a 90° angle or from straight in front of you. Run with the flirt pole instead of walking. Move much farther away, add a stop, and then ask your dog to walk forward again.

Having some fun with Sir playing with our small flirt pole.

Eat, tug, or flirt?

If you have been using treats to play the Green grass games, you now may want to transition to a tug or flirt pole. So how do you go about doing that? If your dog absolutely won't tug, don't worry, I've got you covered. Keep reading!

You can first switch from using treats to using a tug with a long handle. When using a tug, hold the handle and the tug in the same hand. Use your other hand to lead your dog around a small cone circle. Once you mark your dog moving to the indicated position, give a verbal marker such as *yes*, and drop the tug in front of your dog while holding on to the handle. This will be a bit tricky because you will be reaching across your body to drop the tug.

HINT: *If you have a small tug, hold both the tug and the handle in your lead hand, then you can just drop the tug out of that hand after you mark your dog getting to the indicated position.*

Using a flirt pole is super simple for gameplay, much easier than trying to hold on to and deliver a tug to your dog. To use a flirt pole, stand and hold the handle and the squirrel in the same hand. Use your other hand to sweep around to indicate where you want your dog to go. When your dog gets almost to your goal position, mark and drop the squirrel in front of your dog. Then have a short tug session with your dog.

HINT: *If your dog is not trotting, when you drop the tug or squirrel in front of them, drag it away from your dog to get them to chase it. Of course, you will do this after you mark and release your dog to get the toy.*

If you are using a tug or a flirt pole to play the game, you would mark with a word (*yes*), then release your dog to get the toy with a release word (*get it*). You want your dog to always wait for a release word before they grab the toy.

HINT: *As prey in the center of the circle, try using a bowl of treats the lid of which has holes in it. Your dog will smell the treats but the lid stops them from reaching the goodies. The bowl stays unopened while you toss treats to your dog.*

If your dog has not mastered verbal directional cues, you need to go back and work on them. From this point on, it is much easier to verbally cue your dog to circle than to lead them around with your hand. See page 90 for teaching verbal directional cues.

You need to transition to verbal directionals to be able to drop the squirrel on the ground and to step back into the cone circle, as shown in the images on this page.

Sir playing cone squares while I use a flirt pole. Note that I am in the center of the setup and holding the squirrel.

Now the squirrel is on the floor and I am on the perimeter of the cone setup. The bowl of treats with holes in the lid could replace the squirrel on the floor.

Squirrel on the loose

Until now, you have been standing on the inside of the cone square or circle while holding both the flirt pole handle and squirrel in your hand(s). The last variation of this game is to drop the squirrel on the floor and step back between cones. First, lower the squirrel to the floor over several sessions. Once you have the squirrel on the floor at your feet. Start taking a step back toward the perimeter of the cone setup.

HINT: *Once you step away from the squirrel on the floor, be ready to whip it back into your hand if your dog dives into the center of the circle to grab it. An unguarded squirrel is a great temptation for your dog.*

Your dog will probably pay much more attention to the position of the squirrel than to your position. Take another step backward and you should be in line with the cones. Be careful not to trip over a cone as you back up. Now you are on the perimeter or the cone setup holding the handle of the flirt pole. The squirrel is in the center of the cones so it looks like you are fishing with a squirrel as bait.

HINT: *For this game, your dog should stay on the outside of the cone setup at all times. Drop treats or swing the squirrel out to your dog, outside of the cones.*

I don't think I have ever played a flirt pole game with my dogs when I didn't end up laughing. I hope you and your dog get as much fun and satisfaction out of playing these games as my dogs and I have. Enrichment games come in all flavors and varieties. Experiment with the games to find which ones you and your dog really enjoy playing.

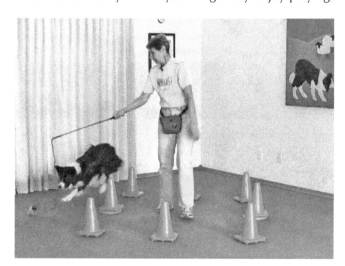

I placed the squirrel on the outside of the cone setup and released Sir to get it.

That's it

Have you noticed that your relationship with your dog is continuing to grow? This growth is due to clear communication with your dog while you both are having fun. I would call that quality time. Isn't quality time what we crave in all of our relationships?

You and your dog have gained some amazing skills. You now have a dog who plays with a flirt pole and has gained some extraordinary self-control. Try using your flirt pole with some of the Green grass games. A flirt pole raises the games to another level as compared to any other reinforcer you may have used before. A flirt pole squirrel beats treats, toys, and tugs, paws down.

Go fish?

Now that you and your dog have mastered many enrichment games, are you up for taking a break to go fishing? Or maybe you and your dog would rather try the Go fish game.

The next game adds flirt pole play to the **Cone circle** game for a combination that puts the fun on steroids.

Cheat sheet #9

Go fish

1. Play Go fish using a long flirt pole with the squirrel on the ground in the center of the circle and you on the perimeter.
2. Change remaining hand signals to verbal cues; stop, arc, and circle.
3. Add flying changes to the game.
4. Use plastic tape to set up a perfect circle by using a central stake and a light line.
5. Play Go Fish with a plastic tape circle.

To win: Dog plays Go Fish while responding to only verbal cues.

Level up: Dog executes flying changes in both directions.

Challenge: _____

_____

_____

CHAPTER 12

Ramping up the fun

This Go fish game is not the Go Fish card game that you played as a kid. This game swaps a flirt pole for a deck of cards and your dog for your best friend, but maybe your dog is your best friend. In that case, the two games are surprisingly similar, but this one happens to be a lot more fun than that old card game from your past.

In this Go fish game, you will be adding a flirt pole to the Cone circle game to rev up the fun. Can you imagine what your dog would be willing to do to get the green light to grab a squirrel?

Callout cues

At this point, you may still be using signals or physical cues to move and stop your dog. You have used a hand sweep to indicate which direction to circle and a drop of your hand to indicate a stop. If you have not already changed from physical to verbal cues as previously instructed, it is now time to up your game! Follow the directions below for switching to verbal cues. To play the Go fish game, you need verbal cues to tell your dog which direction to circle and when to stop.

Fortunately, since you already have body and hand signals in place, it is relatively easy to install verbal cues. Pick cues that are easy for you to remember and are very different from other cues that your dog already knows. My suggestions for these verbal cues are *stop* for stop and *arc* and *circle* for circling.

I always think about circling as if I were looking down at the cone circle from above, the view an overhead drone or bird would have. Thus, I think of the circular directions as clockwise and counterclockwise, or **c**lockwise and **a**nti-clockwise.

HINT: *If you use **arc** and **circle** as your circling cues, you can remember which way is which by associating the first letter of the direction with the first letter of the cue: Arc = Anti-clockwise and Circle = Clockwise*

New cue, old cue

In review, adding a verbal cue should be quite simple since your dog already knows the physical cues for these actions. Let's look at an example of adding the verbal *arc* cue. Once you have added the word cue *arc*, you will no longer have to sweep your hand to tell your dog to move counterclockwise.

Adding a new cue

PART A

1. Set up a cone circle 12 feet in diameter.
2. Grab a toy or treats to toss.
3. Your dog is on the outside of the cone circle facing you.
4. You are in the center of the circle facing your dog.

5. Raise your left hand toward your dog and sweep it out and backward as your dog follows your hand. Your dog will be moving counterclockwise.
6. Move forward in a tight circle until your dog has gone a quarter circle. Mark and toss your toy.
7. Reset your dog.

PART B

1. Repeat asking your dog to circle a quarter circle in the same direction each time.
2. Now say your verbal cue, *arc*, before you move your hand or body.
3. Pause a moment, then raise and sweep your hand and turn your body.

4. Walk forward until your dog has gone another quarter circle.
5. Repeat Part B, using your new verbal cue; pause, then add your old physical cue.

PART C

1. Once your dog starts moving counterclockwise when you give your verbal cue, drop your physical cue. (Turn your body so that you can watch your dog, but don't raise your hand.)

2.   Use your verbal cue five more times to move your dog a quarter circle counterclockwise and end the session.

PART D

1.   Do a few game sessions with your new *arc* cue.
2.   Start over and repeat all of the **Adding a new cue** steps, with your dog circling in the opposite direction to add your new clockwise cue *circle*.

PART E

1.   After your dog is confident taking each verbal circling cue, start mixing them up in the same session. Stop your dog in between circling cues.
2.   Again, get your dog comfortable with the two verbal directional cues, then repeat the procedure and add your verbal stop cue.
3.   Finally, you can mix all of your verbal cues and drop all physical cues.

You use the same basic procedure to add your verbal stop cue as you used to add the directional cues; old physical cue, pause, and then new verbal cue. Once you have your dog stopping on your physical cues, add the word *stop* before physically indicating the stop. When your dog begins to stop when they hear the verbal cue, drop the physical cue or signal.

HINT: *Make sure that you separate the new verbal cue from the old physical cue with a slight pause or your dog will ignore your verbal cue and key on the old physical signal.*

The key to changing a hand signal or body movement cue to a verbal cue is the short pause between the new and old cues. The pause is necessary because dogs find movement more salient or noteworthy than sounds. When verbal and physical cues are delivered very close together, dogs pay attention to physical movement rather than the sound of the spoken word.

HINT: *You may still use some physical prompts to help your dog be successful playing the games. Drop the prompts as your dog progresses.*

Throwing a tug to Sir after he took my verbal cue to stop. Note that I threw the tug outside of the cone circle.

Play the Cone circle game until your dog is confident responding to all of your verbal cues. Now that you have all of your physical cues changed to verbal ones, you are ready to go fishing!

A game of a different color

In the Cone circle game, you added several, or a few, obstacles for your dog to interact with. You may have added foot targets, low jumps, platforms, or whatever else you and your dog fancied. To play the Go fish game, you need to remove all of those obstacles and go back to just a cone circle.

Don't worry, as you play this obstacle-free game, you will soon be ramping up the challenge for your dog and keeping them locked in and thriving. This game combines elements from many of the previous games.

HINT: *If you haven't yet worked with a flirt pole, check out* Chapter 10: The optional game your dog won't want to miss. *You must have all of the flirt pole basics in place before you can start using a flirt pole in games!*

Safety first

Remember to always use an abundance of caution when playing any games with your dog, be particularly vigilant when playing with a flirt pole. Dogs can become determined to get the squirrel on the end of the flirt pole and will jump and twist if the squirrel is slowly flown back into your hand. Keep your dog safe!

HINT: *Use a long flirt pole to play this game. A horse lunge whip with a toy on the end is a perfect long flirt pole.*

Sir grabbing the flirt pole squirrel. Again, note that squirrel is placed to the outside of the cone circle.

HINT: *In place of a flirt pole squirrel, try placing a bowl of treats covered with a lid with holes in it in the center of the circle. The lid will allow your dog to smell the treats but will prevent them from helping themselves to the treats.*

You can play the Go fish game without using a flirt pole. Make sure that whatever reinforcer you leave in the center of the circle is not available for your dog to grab and use to self-reinforce when you are not standing near it. Be creative! You might use a ball on a rope or a tug with a long handle so that you can snatch the toy away before your dog can get to it.

HINT: *Remember, in the Go fish game, all of the reinforcement is tossed or presented to your dog on the outside of the cone circle.*

Using a covered bowl of treats in the center of your circle is not ideal. Most dogs have prey drive; if a toy or tug is attached to a light line and pulled along the ground away from them, they will try to grab it – this desire can be shaped into tugging. Never drag the toy or tug toward your dog since prey escapes by running away. If you bring the toy toward your dog, it is as if the prey is challenging your dog and your dog may feel intimidated. You want to boost your dog's confidence, not erode it, so always have the "prey" run away from your dog.

Flirt pole use – Go fish game

PART A

1. Set up a cone circle 12 feet in diameter.
2. Stand in the center of the circle facing your dog.
3. Hold the flirt pole handle in one hand and the squirrel in the other.
4. Verbally cue your dog to circle clockwise.

5. When your dog has traveled a quarter of the way around the circle, mark and flip the squirrel out in front of your dog. Have a short tug session.
6. Move your dog back and forth in random directions a quarter circle for each cue given until your dog is confidently taking your cues. (You can send your dog any direction around the circle, random direction choices work best.)

PART B

1. Lower the squirrel from your waist to your knees. (This won't seem like a big deal to you but your dog will probably notice the change.)
2. Repeat Part A with the squirrel at knee level.

PART C

1. Now lower the squirrel to the ground. (It will still be close to your feet.)
2. Repeat Part A with the squirrel on the ground.

PART D

1. Take a step back toward the cone circle while leaving the squirrel on the ground in the center of the circle. (**Be alert**: your dog may decide to grab the squirrel as you are no longer standing near it.)
2. When ready, take another step backward toward the cone circle.

3. Eventually, you will be standing in line with the cone circle and the squirrel will be in the center of the circle.
4. Repeat Part A with the squirrel in the center of the circle while you stand on the perimeter of the circle. Ta da: you are playing the Go fish game!

Although it is called the Go fish game, you don't have to hold the shaft of your flirt pole pointed up, as you would a fishing rod. You can hold the flirt pole so that the shaft points to or touches the ground.

HINT: *Remember that if you have the shaft of your flirt pole touching the ground, you will have to raise it much farther to whip the squirrel back into your hand than if it is already pointed upward.*

Flying changes

Flying changes are when your dog changes direction while circling, but without stopping. Flying changes of direction are easy for your dog to learn and they look quite impressive when performed at speed.

Sir doing a flying change of direction.

NOTE: *If your dog isn't very agile or has structure or health issues, skip flying changes. Always use your best judgement when playing the games. There is no traditional winning or losing in these games. You and your dog win when you have fun together as you grow closer.*

Flying change of direction

PART A

1. Set up your standard cone circle and grab your long flirt pole.
2. Circle your dog slowly in either direction a quarter circle. (If your dog is going slow, they are more likely to be successful when you first ask for a direction change without a stop between directional cues, which will happen soon.)
3. Stop your dog.

4. Send your dog slowly in the opposite direction a quarter circle.
5. Stop your dog.

6. Repeat this change of directions, with a stop between direction changes, several times.

PART B

1. Repeat Part A, but don't stop your dog to have them change directions.
2. If your dog successfully flips around and heads in the opposite direction, mark and pop out the squirrel to your dog and have a huge celebration!
3. If your dog keeps going in the same direction instead of reversing directions, stop your dog and repeat Part A again.
4. When your dog is successfully changing from one direction to the other, try the opposite directional change. (If your dog has mastered *arc* to *circle*, start on *circle* to *arc* while repeating Part A again.)

PART C

1. Eventually, throw in flying changes of direction randomly and at speed.
2. Add flying changes to your tape circle setup. (Don't know what a "tape circle setup" is? Read on!)

Lifelines

- **Dog struggles with flying changes** – Ask for a change of direction as soon as your dog starts to circle. The faster your dog gets moving, the more difficult it is for them to change directions or do any cued behavior.
- **Dog struggles with flying changes in one direction** – If your dog has trouble changing directions without a stop in one direction, but easily completes flying changes in the other direction, concentrate on the flying change to the troublesome side and ignore the other side for a few sessions.

High-energy dogs love quick movement and flying changes are right up their alleys. Most active dogs are quite agile and can flip around and head in the opposite direction with ease.

HINT: *Safety first, last, and always when playing together!*

Tape circle setup

A tape or plastic tape circle setup is perfect for the Go fish game. Tape comes in many colors and widths, is not adhesive, and usually is on a cardboard roll. I use yellow tape, 3 inches wide. Tape can be found in hardware/tool or home improvement stores.

Setting up a tape circle setup is optional, but it looks really cool! You will need some type of stakes to hold the tape above the ground. If you use cones with holes in them you could thread the plastic tape through the holes, if they are the appropriate height. The level of your dog's elbow is a good height for a tape circle.

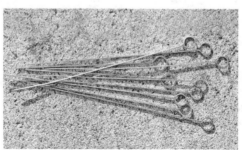

Roll of plastic tape.   *Shish kabob skewers.*

Using a tape circle can also come in handy as an intermediate step for keeping your dog on the perimeter. If your dog keeps wanting to come in to you after you remove your original see-through barrier, a tape circle may be a great option for you.

There are many options for holding up the plastic tape. You can attach it to the top of your cones or thread it through holes in your cones. You can also use wooden stakes or shish kabob skewers to hold up the tape.

Circle of tape on skewers.

HINT: *It is easier for dogs to see yellow than red so grab yellow tape if you have a choice between yellow and red.*

Sir running around a tape circle with jumps and foot targets.

Go fish is the ideal game to play using plastic tape circles and long flirt poles. As you will see, you can also add other obstacles around the outside of the circle to enhance your play.

HINT: *To set up a perfect circle, place a stake where the center of the circle will be. Then attach a string to the stake and use it as a guide to place cones or stakes to hold the plastic tape. Remove the center stake and string when finished.*

Setting up a cone setup using a stake and a light line.

In the next game, Level up, you will be asking your dog to come into the center of the circle so tape circles are not suitable for that game. In the meantime, feel free to set up a tape circle, add some obstacles and go fish.

Cheat sheet #10

Level up

1. Polish speed changes and add to games.
2. Set up the environment so that backing up comes naturally to your dog.
3. Dog backs out from under a chair.
4. Dog continues backing once clear of the chair.
5. Dog backs away from a target.
6. Move target around the game area.
7. Add speed changes and moving forward and back to the game.

To win: Dog changes speed, goes faster or slower, when cued.

Level up: Dog moves forward and back when cued.

Challenge: _____

_____

_____

CHAPTER 13

Ready to level up?

Now that the **Go fish** game is easy for you and your dog, it's time to level up or move to the next level of play! Introducing the **Level up** game. This game adds a few new elements to get your dog moving not only around the circle but into and back out of it.

In addition to these new movements, you may want to throw in some transitions between elements to keep your dog guessing. This game will get your dog moving at different speeds and in new directions; faster and slower and forward and back. Are you and your dog ready for the challenge?

On the level

The **Level up** game uses essentially the same cone circle setup as the **Go fish** game. If you used plastic tape for the circle boundary of that game, you will need to switch over to a cone circle. You should only use plastic tape for games when your dog stays out on the perimeter of the circle.

HINT: *You don't want your dog jumping over a plastic-tape boundary as they could trip and injure themselves.*

You will be using a flirt pole or other reinforcers such as a tug or treats for this game. To keep your dog thinking and engaged, we will add a few new movements and changes of direction to this game.

Get up to speed

A fun way to switch things up is to ask your dog to move faster or slower as they move around the circle. Initially, use hand signals. Later, you will switch to verbal cues. Many dogs will adjust their speed to the movement of your hand. As your hand moves faster they increase their speed and as your hand movement slows down, they slow down.

Set up a 6-foot cone circle, inside if you have room, and grab some treats that you can toss on the floor for your dog. To start, you will only be asking your dog to speed up from a walk to a trot and to slow down from a trot to a walk. Later you can move outside, increase the size of your cone circle, and introduce changing speeds from a trot to a canter and from a canter back down to a trot.

HINT: *Pick a time when your dog is not overly excited or they will likely want to run around the circle rather than walk or trot.*

Start this game by asking your dog to increase their circling speed from a walk to a trot. You can substitute changing from a trot to a canter if your dog is more active. Read through the entire game plan before you start and adapt it to suit your dog. To encourage your dog to speed up, you can trot in a small circle and use happy words, while you quickly sweep your hand. To slow your dog down from a trot to a walk: slow your movements, calm your voice, and decrease the speed of your sweeping hand.

HINT: *Keep your dog circling in the same direction for the entire **Speed change – walk to trot** game plan below.*

Speed change – walk to trot

PART A

1. Set up a cone circle 6 feet in diameter and grab some treats that you can toss.
2. Stand in the center of the circle facing your dog.
3. Your dog will be on the outside of the circle, facing you.
4. Extend one hand toward your dog and indicate the direction you want your dog to travel around the circle.
5. If your dog starts to canter or trot as they circle, stop, drop your hand, and wait for your dog to stop. Reset your dog and begin again.

6. If your dog walks, take your dog halfway around the circle and stop.
7. Ask your dog to walk another half circle in the same direction.
8. Stop your dog.

PART B

1. Ask your dog to circle again and, as they circle, ask them to speed up from a walk to a trot by saying *chit-chit* or *hurry* in a happy voice. You can trot in a small circle and sweep your hand a bit faster as prompts for your dog. (I find that using a chit-chit cue naturally encourages my dog to move faster. Remember to use your verbal cue first and then add physical prompts.)
2. When your dog starts to trot, mark and then toss a treat slightly ahead of them.
3. Reset and repeat until your dog is moving from a walk to a trot when you cue them, either with your verbal cue or a hand signal.

4. Start adding a verbal cue: *chit-chit*, *hurry*, or *let's go* before your hand signal or body movement.
5. Play this game until your dog is consistently moving from a walk to a trot, with only a verbal cue.

6. Restart Part A and have your dog circle in the opposite direction.
7. Celebrate and take a long break! (Do several sessions of having your dog speed up before you start asking them to slow down in Part C.)

PART C

1. Now it is time to get your dog slowing down from a trot to a walk.
2. Continue using treats and the same-sized cone circle.
3. Get your dog set up as you stand in the center of the circle.
4. Start your dog moving around the circle at a trot. If your dog walks, cue them to start trotting.
5. Now ask your dog to slow back down to a walk by saying *easy* or *slowly* in a soft, calm voice. Slow your movement. (Verbal cue, then physical prompt.)

6. As soon as your dog changes from trotting to walking, mark and then hand your dog a treat.
7. Reset your dog and repeat Part C until your dog will drop from a trot to a walk when verbally cued.

8. Restart Part C and have your dog circle in the opposite direction.
9.   Work slowing down in both directions and take a well-deserved break!

Lifelines

- **Dog will not walk around the circle** – With some high-energy dogs, you may have to start playing this game at a faster gait. Instead of moving from a walk to a trot, you may have to start at a trot and have your dog move up to a canter.
- **Dog will only canter around the circle** – Start by playing the game at a canter and ask your dog to slow to a trot. Then ask your dog to move from a trot to a canter before working on the walk/trot transitions.
- **Dog will only canter around the circle** – Expand your circle diameter to 12 feet and allow your dog to circle a few times to expend some energy before you ask them to slow to a trot.

When your dog has their walk/trot transitions on cue, move on to trot/canter transitions. Enlarge the diameter of your circle to 12 feet and then follow the *Speed change – walk to trot game plan* above substituting trot for walk and canter for trot in the plan. Once your dog is a pro at moving faster and slower when cued, it is time to move on to some flirt pole play.

Walk in to flirt

Your dog was introduced to flirt pole play in Chapters 10, 11, and 12. In those chapters the stop, grab, and walk toward the toy squirrel were covered. If you and your dog need a refresher on those games, head back to Chapter 10 and play your way through the games again. If you are good to go, onward!

This game plan uses a 12-foot cone circle and toy prey or a food target in the center of the circle. I like to stand on the perimeter of the circle holding a long flirt pole handle with the squirrel in the circle's center. You can also place a toy or covered food bowl in the center of the circle as a target.

Sir walking in toward a squirrel in the center of the circle.

Do you have a cue?

Your dog should already know all of the verbal cues that you will use in this game. Since this game gets a bit more complicated, it might be a good time to review all of the cues you are now using. The cues your dog should know include: *walk, stop, arc, circle, hurry, easy,* and *get it*. You may use these exact words or other words that you have chosen as your verbal cues. Head back to page 90 to add verbal cues.

HINT: *Feel free to change a verbal cue to a different cue if you decide your dog needs to relearn a behavior. Teach the new behavior and then add a totally new verbal cue to it.*

Your dog should also be coming to you when cued as well as taking and releasing a toy on cue. As you can see, you and your dog have gained a tremendous amount of new skills with new cues. Bravo! Hopefully, gaining these skills has been fun and easy. As you and your dog have gained skills, you may have also noticed that your communication and relationship have both improved. Big win.

Back off

Walking backward may be new to your dog. Most dogs don't spend much, if any time, moving backward since a dog doesn't have much need to walk backward in their everyday life. Thus, your first step is to teach your dog that they can walk backward.

There are several ways to get your dog to offer backing up. You can lean into or over your dog to push them backward, but that can be intimidating for your dog. Instead, think about how you could set up the environment so that backing up comes naturally to your dog.

Sit down for success

It is fun to watch your dog figure out that they can walk backward. This game makes backing up not only the correct answer but also your dog's most natural response. Another win-win. I love win-wins!

Sir going under a chair to get a treat.

All that you need to play this game are some treats and a chair with a seat high enough that your dog can put their head under it. Try to use a chair that your dog can easily get their head under without having to crouch down or crawl.

The game plan for **Back up** may look daunting but its simple steps can be quickly completed. I have broken down the plan to make it clear and easy for you and your dog.

I suggest you read through the entire game plan before you start so that you know where you and your dog are heading. Feel free to jump ahead in the plan if your dog catches on without needing all of the steps.

Back up from under a chair

PART A

1. Grab a handful of yummy treats and sit down on your chair. Place your feet out to the side and in front of the legs of the chair.
2. Your dog will be standing in front of and facing you.
3. Place a treat on the floor between you and your dog and release your dog to eat the treat off of the floor.
4. Keep placing treats, one at a time, closer to your chair. Allow your dog to snarf up each treat before you place the next one.

---

5. When your dog is close to the front of your chair, reach under the seat of the chair and place a treat just under the chair. Your dog will then have to duck their head under the chair to get the treat.
6. Start placing treats farther under the chair.

---

7. While your dog is ducked under the seat of the chair, they will eat the treat you placed there and then step back to look at you. Mark your dog stepping backward (yes) and feed another treat.
8. Repeat by placing a treat far under your chair, then marking your dog as they back out.

---

9. Feed a treat once your dog is standing facing you again.
10. Repeat until your dog is comfortable backing out from under your chair and take a break.

PART B

1. Place a treat under your chair as you did in Part A three times, marking your dog backing up and then feeding another treat.
2. Next, place a treat as usual, but this time don't mark your dog as they back out from under the chair. Instead, wait. Your dog will back out and look at you. Watch your dog and wait to see if they will offer to back up one step.
3. If your dog offers a step backward, mark, treat, and celebrate.
4. If your dog just looks at you, try placing a treat between their front feet such that they have to take a step back to eat the treat.

5. Repeat until you get one step back a few times. (This step backward comes when your dog is standing in front of you, not when they are moving their head out from under your chair.)
6. Quit for the day and really celebrate! Your dog is realizing that they can walk backward!

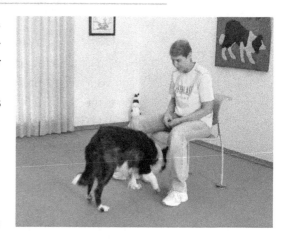

Sir backing out from under a chair.

PART C

1. Sit in your chair and have your dog stand and face you.
2. Pause for a moment and see if your dog will offer a step back.
3. If your dog takes a step back, mark and place or toss a treat between their front feet. Be ready to mark and toss another treat as your dog takes another step back. After your dog has taken a few steps backward, call them to you and start again.
4. If your dog just stands and looks at you, repeat Part B above.

5. When your dog is backing 3 to 5 steps, with a treat tossed to them between each step, start waiting for your dog to offer a second step.
6. Now mark and treat your dog for backing 2 steps instead of just one step.

7. Ping pong the number of steps that your dog takes before you mark and treat.
8. Over several sessions you will have your dog backing 3 to 5 steps for one mark and treat.

PART D

1. Once your dog is confidently backing up 3 to 5 steps it is time to add a verbal cue such as *back*.
2. Sit in your chair and set your dog up as usual. Wait for them to back up a few steps. Call your dog to you, feed a treat, and give your verbal cue just as your dog finishes eating the treat and hopefully before they start backing up again.

3. Repeat until your dog is backing when cued.
4. Take a break for a huge celebration!
5. Repeat Part D a few times over several days.

PART E

1. Now, pick up a tug or toy and place it on your lap. (You are still sitting in a chair.) Cue your dog to back away from you and the toy. Repeat 5 times.
2. Place the toy on the floor between your feet and have your dog back away. Repeat 5 times.
3. Now stand with the toy on the floor between your feet and have your dog back away. Repeat 5 times.

4. Remove the chair and stand. Place the toy on the floor between your feet and have your dog back away. Repeat 5 times. (From now on, repeat each step 5 times.)
5. Incrementally step back from and off to the side of the toy. (Your dog should now be backing away from the toy and not from you.)

6. Move the toy around the room, a few feet at a time. Be sure to use your verbal cue, mark, and then feed a treat to your dog for backing away from the toy.
7. Awesome! Your dog now knows how to back away from a target when cued!

You can change the target from a toy to a bowl of treats or a squirrel by placing a new target next to the old one. Have your dog back away from both targets for a session or two. Then remove the old target and leave just the new target. Your dog will now be backing away from only the new target. Yay!

Lifelines

- **Dog is afraid to go under the chair** – Try a different chair such as a plastic lawn chair or a tall stool.
- **Dog is afraid to go under the chair** – Try standing in a hallway, spread your feet apart and place the treat in front of you. Then move the treat under you

and eventually under and behind you. (You may need to place a barrier a few feet behind you to prevent your dog from walking through your legs instead of backing out from under you.)

- **Dog isn't catching on to backing** – Sit on a cushion on the floor with your dog standing facing you. Try placing a treat between and slightly behind your dog's front feet. Be ready to mark and then place another treat as your dog steps backward to eat the first treat. Jump into Part B step 4 in the plan above. Follow the rest of the game plan while sitting on the floor.
- **Dog got stuck or confused** – Go back to a step that is easy for your dog and start from there. This time, repeat the steps as many times as necessary until you see your dog gain confidence. Then move on to the next step.
- **Dog got stuck or confused** – Try teaching the back using the alternate target mat approach on the next page. I have had a lot of success using this method, so give it a try if your dog is stuck.

HINT: *If you get confused as you play this game, stop playing. Reread the steps and go back to the last step that you and your dog were successfully playing. Pick up the game at that step and take your time moving forward. Alternatively, try a different approach that is better suited to your dog, such as back to the mat as taught below.*

Back to the mat

Another way to teach back is to use a target mat. Use a fairly large mat with a different texture from the surface you are working on. I find carpet remnants make good target mats. Be sure the target does not slip around on the surface you are working on.

Back up to a target mat

PART A

1. Grab a handful of yummy treats.
2. Place a mat on the floor and position your dog with their rear feet on the mat. You will be standing directly in front of your dog.
3. Feed several treats while your dog stands with only their rear feet on the mat.
4. Pull your dog toward you by luring with a treat or patting your leg such that *one* of their rear feet moves forward and off of the mat. (You may need to take a step backward to get your dog to move toward you.)

5. Look at the mat and wait for your dog to place their rear paw back onto the mat.
6. Mark your dog's rear paw stepping back onto the mat.

7. Repeat until your dog immediately moves their rear paw back onto the mat as soon as they step off of it.

PART B

1. Now start pulling your dog toward you such that *both* of their rear feet move forward and off of the mat.
2. Look at the mat and wait for your dog to place one rear paw back onto the mat.
3. Mark your dog's rear paw stepping onto the mat.

4. Repeat until your dog immediately moves one rear paw back onto the mat as soon as they step off of it.
5. Now, withhold your mark until your dog places both rear paws back onto the mat.

6. Repeat until your dog immediately moves both rear paws back onto the mat as soon as they step off of it.

PART C

1. Take a step backward and pull your dog farther off of the mat.
2. Mark as your dog places both rear feet on the mat.

3. Ping pong the distance you pull your dog off of the mat.
4. Continue to mark as your dog places both rear feet on the mat.
5. Extend the distance your dog backs to the mat, 3 to 5 steps.

6. Remove the mat and mark when your dog has backed 3 steps.
7. Increase the distance your dog backs before the mark to 4 to 5 steps.

PART D

1. Once your dog is confidently backing up 3 to 5 steps it is time to add a verbal cue such as *back*.
2. Set your dog up as usual. Wait for them to back up a few steps. Call your dog to you, feed a treat, and give your verbal cue just as your dog finishes eating the treat and hopefully before they start backing again.

3. Repeat until your dog is backing when cued.

4. Take a break for a huge celebration!
5. Repeat **Part D** a few times over several days.

PART E

1. Now, pick up a tug or toy and place it on the floor between your feet.
2. Cue your dog to back away from you and the toy. Repeat 5 times. (From now on, repeat each step 5 times.)
3. Incrementally step back from and off to the side of the toy. (Your dog should now be backing away from the toy and not from you.)

4. Move the toy around the room, a few feet at a time. Be sure to use your verbal cue, mark, and then feed a treat to your dog for backing away from the toy.
5. Awesome! Your dog now knows how to back away from a target when cued!

Sir stepping back to the target mat.

I taught the back while sitting in a chair, but standing allows you much more freedom of movement. You need to move to pull your dog farther and farther from the mat.

Sir backing up a few steps to the target mat.

To repeat, you can change the target from a toy to a bowl of treats, a different toy, or a squirrel by placing the new target beside the old one. Have your dog back away from both targets for a session or two. Then remove the old target and leave just the new target. Your dog will now be backing away from only the new target. Yay!

Your dog is so smart! They now can speed up, slow down, walk in, and back up on cue! You always knew your dog was brilliant but now the whole world will know. Absolutely fantastic!

Sir backing away from a squirrel.

Game on!

You are now ready to add these four new behaviors to the Level up game. Start out adding either speeding up and slowing down or walking toward and backing away from a target.

HINT: *Don't add all of your dog's new tricks at once.*

Add the easier part of a new pair of behaviors first and later add the part that your dog struggles with. Having success with one part will set your dog up to have success with the part they initially struggled with.

A mixed bag

Finally, once your dog has mastered all of the parts of this game, you can level up one more time. Really! The final level of this game has your dog transitioning from faster to slower or from walking in to backing up without stopping between actions. Be sure to also add circling into the Level up game.

A game session might include a sequence or string of cues such as: *circle, stop, walk in, back, arc, hurry,* and *stop.* Start out with simple, very short sequences of behaviors and increase the game's complexity over time. Always make things simple for your dog and then ramp up the level of play. Be sure to provide plenty of play that is easy for your dog or you may take the fun out of the games. If you find you are not laughing as you play the game, then it is probably no longer fun for your dog either.

Sir playing Level Up in the summer.

Sir playing Level up in the winter.

Both humans and dogs like to be challenged. Challenges can be exciting if they are achievable and don't continually become more and more difficult. Adjust the level of challenge, either up or down, to where you and your dog are comfortable on any specific day. Life happens.

There also may be days that you simply don't want to play games. That's okay. Give yourself and your dog a break knowing that you are both doing the best you can. At times, taking a necessary break can go just as far in building a great relationship as playing a fun game can.

It's not the playing together that builds an awesome relationship, it's the respect you give to yourself and your dog as you meet each other's needs. As you explore the last enrichment game, Blue sky, you will find unlimited options for growing your relationship with your dog while meeting your and your dog's wants and needs.

Cheat sheet #11

Blue sky

1. Design your own personal games combining elements from any enrichment game.
2. Safety first, fun always!
3. Two dogs can play at once.
4. Play with two circles, side by side.
5. Try three-circle play in a triangular setup.
6. Add transitions from circle to circle.
7. Add off-circle obstacles.
8. Dream on ...

To win: Design a game using your and your dog's favorite game elements.

Level up: Create unique, special game elements to add to your personal game.

Challenge: _____

_____

_____

CHAPTER 14

Blue sky and beyond

The **Blue sky** game is the pinnacle of enrichment games. This game fosters the creation of an unlimited number of new, personalized games. Use your favorite obstacles in unique configurations for a truly one-of-a-kind experience. Game setups are limited only by your imagination. If you can dream it, you can play it!

You can design games that range from Homemade Vanilla to Salted Caramel Chocolate Galaxy. Well, maybe skip the chocolate for your dog's sake. Pretty much any flavor of game that you and your dog want to play is possible.

HINT: *Only safety sets a limit to your creativity as you imagine new games.*

One dog, two dog
How about playing a game with both of your dogs at the same time? Definitely a possibility. Introduce each dog to the game setup individually. Once both dogs are proficient playing alone, they can start playing together. Of course, safety would be uppermost in your mind. Both dogs would have to be physically capable of playing the game and get along so that they played nicely. No squabbling allowed!

Freestyle
Think of the **Blue sky** game as a freestyle-type framework for designing games that suit you and your dog. Games that showcase your and your dog's special talents, skills, and style. Games that enhance and reveal the no-regrets relationship that you and your dog share.

Take games that you and your dog have previously enjoyed, add an exciting twist or two, and you have a Blue sky game. A game that is new, unique, and totally personalized for you and your dog.

Three-ring circus

You and your dog may have played enrichment games with both cone circles and plastic-tape circles. Consider how you might set up a game using multiple circles or rings. The important consideration when deciding on which type of circle to use is: Do you want your dog to enter the center of the circle as part of this game? If your dog is going to enter the circle, then use cone circles. If your dog is not going to enter the circle, then you are free to use either cone or plastic-tape circles.

 HINT: *Your circles don't have to be completely circular, they can be a bit oval-shaped to fit your preference or play area limitations.*

The limiting factor may be how many cones or other equipment you have on hand. If you set up two or three rings, you can use a different perimeter marker for each circle. Let's look at a few circle setups to give you an idea of the possibilities.

Sneak peeks

So what might a Blue sky circle setup look like? Two basic ring setups come to mind; two circles side-by-side and three circles that form a triangle.

First, let's look at two circles side by side. I like to use different cones for each circle or use one circle of cones and one of plastic tape. At first, you may have to put the circles quite a distance apart to help your dog stay on the circle you are indicating.

Initially, you may want to stop your dog between the circles to transition from one circle to the other. Work the first circle in both directions before moving to the second circle. This allows your dog to get comfortable moving around each circle before you ask them to move from circle to circle.

After you and your dog are confident playing with two circles, you may want to add a third. Again, I suggest you make the circles out of different colored cones or a combination of plastic tape and cones, but the main thing is to work each circle separately until you and your dog are confidently playing on each.

Two circles side-by-side.

Three circles that form a triangle.

You may be limited by the number of cones you have or the area you have to set up circles. Don't worry if you only have room for one circle. You can add an unlimited variety of obstacles around the circle as well as have your dog come into and back out of the circle. You can also up the ante by asking your dog to slow down and speed up, as well as move in and back out of the circle.

HINT: *Look back through all of the Enrichment games, grab elements from any game, and add them to your Blue sky setup.*

Of course, you can add more complexity and precision by putting your circling and other behaviors on verbal cues. Things can get challenging as you add more obstacles, off-circle obstacles, behaviors, and circles, so proceed slowly.

Turning point

A turning point is the place where your dog moves from one circle to another, a decision point for your dog. At this point your dog either continues around the current circle or moves to another circle. You want to introduce turning points to your dog before you ask them to play a game with two or more circles.

The turning point is just before the midway point between two adjacent circles. At the turning point, you tell your dog which path to take; either continue circling the circle they are currently on or switch to the new circle.

Standing between circles

For circles near each other there are two options. For the first option, you would stand between the two circles and face the circle your dog is moving around. If using a flirt pole, the squirrel would be in the center of that circle. As long as you want your dog to continue on that circle you would maintain that position.

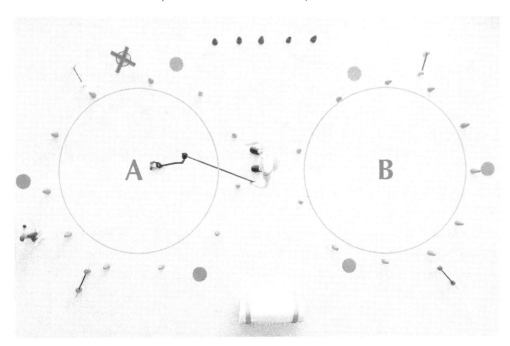

The switching point is marked with an orange X. When your dog gets to this point you would turn and face the other circle and flip the flirt pole squirrel to the other circle.

When you want your dog to switch to the other circle, wait until your dog is reaching the switching point (orange X) then turn your body to face the other circle. Once your dog is used to switching between two circles, you can add a third circle.

You will follow the same procedure for changing circles. Face one circle, then turn to face the next circle and sweep your hand toward the new circle. Alternately, flip the squirrel to the center of the next circle, if you are using a flirt pole.

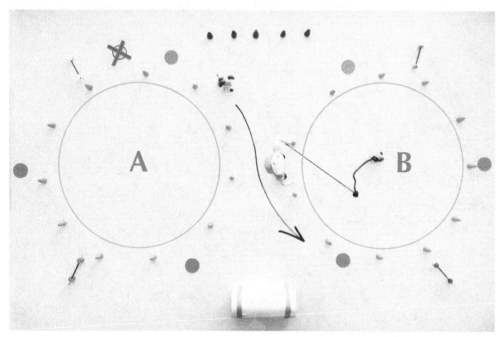

If using a flirt pole, you would flip the squirrel into the center of the other circle as you turned your body. (Your dog would pass behind you as they switched to the new circle.)

HINT: *Have your dog moving no faster than a trot when you start switching circles. Later your dog will be switching from one circle to another at speed.*

Switching circles takes a bit of practice, for you and your dog. Start out slow and experiment to see what works and what doesn't. There are no hard and fast rules. You need to adjust the turning point to suit your and your dog's needs. Always feel free to stop your dog to switch circles and plan to stop your dog if you are switching using tape circles.

Standing in the center of circles

The other circle transition option is to move from the center of one circle to the center of the other circle to indicate when and where your dog is to switch from one circle to the other.

Using this method you physically walk from the center of one circle to the center of the other circle, well before you want your dog to switch from one circle to the next. How soon you need to move depends on the speed your dog is traveling. The faster they are moving, the sooner you will need to walk to the center of the other circle.

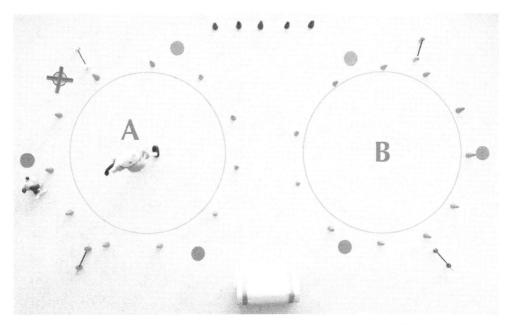

*If you are standing in the center of a circle, the switching point (**orange X**) is farther from where the circles touch so that you have time to walk to the center of the other circle before your dog gets to the turning point.*

HINT: *Switching between circles can be confusing for you and your dog. Your dog will need time to get comfortable with transitions.*

Start with your dog moving slowly to determine exactly when you need to begin moving from one circle to the next. Also, if you are going to move between circles, be sure to use cone circles as much as possible since crossing plastic tape circles may cause you to trip. Once you and your dog are comfortable playing with a two-circle setup, you can then move on to a three-circle setup.

HINT: *As stated many times, keep safety uppermost in your mind at all times. If you or your dog gets injured, it is no fun at all!*

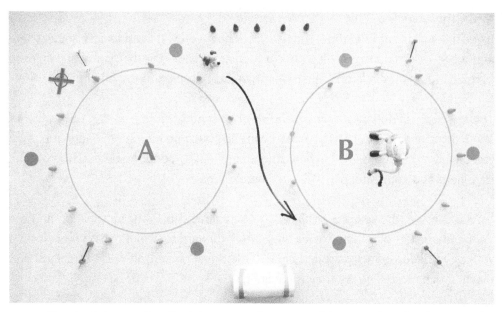

You don't have to be all of the way to the center of the second circle when your dog changes to the new circle. Turn, face your dog, and guide them with an outstretched hand to give them the idea of changing circles.

Blue sky and beyond

Multiple dogs, multiple circles – what else is there? The sky is the limit! Now that your dog is able to play with a two-circle setup, how about adding some new off-circle obstacles that pull your dog off of one circle to get to the next circle?

Off-circle obstacles may affect transitions or turning points. Do a bit of experimentation to determine where your new turning points are located. If you use an off-circle obstacle that has an associated verbal cue, give your cue at the turning point to send your dog to the off-circle obstacle. Off-circle obstacles that your dog may already have cues for include jumps, foot targets, or tunnels.

Two circles with off-circle obstacles; tunnel and low jumps.

Walk this way

If you are walking around the setup with your dog, you will need to determine where and when to position yourself to make it clear to your dog that you want them to transition to an off-circle obstacle rather than just transition to the other circle.

There are tons of options for where and when to send your dog, so start out with your dog moving at a slow pace. As you and your dog become more competent at playing together, the transitions will become smooth and easy. Spend the time to iron out the transitions and your gameplay will become effortless.

As you can see, the setup possibilities are only limited by your imagination and the skills and abilities of you and your dog. I look forward to seeing what you come up with as you add obstacles around circles, additional circles, off-circle obstacles, and much, much more. The sky truly is the limit!

That's a wrap!

You and your dog now have some amazing skills that will enable you to play an endless variety of enrichment games. My hope is that by playing these games you come to an even greater appreciation of just how amazing your dog is and how limited the amount of time is that you have to share with your special friend.

Don't waste precious moments worrying that you or your dog aren't perfect. Instead, spend your time enriching your and your dog's lives by spending fun time together; be it a quiet walk, a trip to compete in a dog sport, or playing a game.

Best wishes as you play your way to a no-regrets relationship with your high-energy dog.

The end: Game over? Circle back!

This is the end of the book, but only the beginning of the possibilities. Now is the time to circle back to the first game, Run the bases, and fill in the Challenge blank. I told you we would circle back!

Who wants to leave a blank blank? It is time to start filling in all of those blank challenge lines by adding new features to each game that you include expressly for you and your dog. Each game can become fresh and new again, the Blue sky version of a familiar game has almost infinite variations. The sky truly is the limit!

Acknowledgments

Psycho border collies – it's tough to live with them and impossible to live without them. I know because I have lived with over a dozen of them through the years.

Of all of the animals that I have worked with over the years – including horses, cats, chickens, geese, sheep, cattle, pigs, and many breeds of dogs – the most difficult and amazing animals to live with have been my border collies.

My dogs have given me unconditional love and patiently tolerated me even when I lost patience with them. They happily played my silly games and provided comfort when I needed it. I loved them one and all.

Besides my dogs, several people have been instrumental in bringing this book to publication. My best friend and unwavering supporter is my husband Kerry. He has heard more "dog talk" than any reasonable husband would tolerate, and listened with a smile.

Thanks to my editors' extraordinaire, Sally Adam and Jane Roznovsky. I also want to thank Jo-Anne Friedlander for her creative suggestions that made this book shine. As a team, you all helped me take this book to the next level. I appreciated all of your suggestions, even the ones I ignored.

And finally, thanks to you my reader and friend for your time and attention. May all of your dogs be as good as Gold.

BB
Purdin
May 2023

About the author

I am a farmer, dog trainer, writer, wife and mother, and border collie lover. I have trained one guiding eye puppy, a few obedience dogs, and many herding dogs over several decades.

But I had to learn how to play with my dogs. As a traditional trainer, training was a very serious business. It was also often frustrating and disheartening. I learned to do it well, but I felt there had to be a better way.

When I found positive training, a whole new world opened up to me and my dogs. This training was simple, but definitely not easy. As I learned my way around the positive world I created games to teach skills to my dogs.

These are the games that I have shared with you in this book. These games will help you and your dog grow and develop into a solid team, just as they helped me and my dogs. Teams that have enviable skills and strong relationships.

These games are ones I have taught to my puppies and played with my old dogs. I have trained chickens to do agility and cows to come when called. All that I have learned about training and playing with animals has come together in this book.

Let the games continue!

Books

Barney, Carolyn. 2007. *Clicker Basics for Dogs and Puppies*.

Book, Mandy & Cheryl Smith. 2001. *Quick Clicks: 40 Fast and Fun Behaviors to Train with a Clicker*.

Clothier, Suzanne. 2002. *Bones Would Rain from the Sky: Deepening Our Relationship with Dogs*.

Fisher, Gail. 2009. *The Thinking Dog: Crossover to Clicker Training*.

Pryor, Karen. 2009. *Reaching the Animal Mind: Clicker Training and What It Teaches Us about All Animals*.

Courses

https://enrichmentgames.com/eg-course

Enrichment games: Green Grass games

Enrichment games: Blue Sky games

Facebook Group

https://www.facebook.com/groups/1319238122176989

Enrichment Games for High-Energy Dogs

Website

www.enrichmentgames.com

Spread the word

I wish you many years of fun play and delightful companionship with your dog. My hope is that this book helps you build the loving relationship you want with your dog.

If you and your dog enjoyed the games in this book, I would appreciate your help in spreading the word by posting a book review on Amazon, Goodreads, or other sites. Your review will help others find this book and determine if it is a good fit for them and their dog.

Even if you haven't finished reading the entire book or haven't played all of the games, please post a review of your experience with the book to date. You can always go back and update your review in the future.

Thanks again and happy playing!

Printed in the USA
CPSIA information can be obtained
at www.ICGtesting.com
CBHW081017280624
10810CB00008B/47